TOMAS POLAK

WITH JIRI RAJLICH

Colour artwork : Malcolm Laird

Layout & project design : Phil Listemann

Copyright © Tomas Polak and Phil Listemann 2008

ISBN 978-295-26-3815-9

Edited by Phil H. Listemann
philedition@wanadoo.fr
www.raf-in-combat.com

Printed in France by
GRAPHIC SUD
BP44 - ZAC de Rigoulet
47552 Boé Cedex, France
Tél : (33).5.53.48.20.30 - Fax : (33).5.53.48.20.35
igs@wanadoo.fr

ACKNOWLEDGEMENTS

C.J. Ehrengardt, Jim Grant (Text Consultant), Malcolm Laird, Andy Thomas, Pavel Vancata.

GLOSSARY OF TERMS

AACU : Anti-Aircraft Cooperation Unit
ADF : Aircraft Delivery Flight
ADGB : Air Defense of Great Britain
ADU : Aircraft Delivery Unit
AFC : Air Force Cross
AFDU : Air Fighting Development Unit
AGS : Advanced Gunnery School
ALG : Advanced Landing Ground
APC : Armament Practice Camp
Armée de l'Air : French Air Force
CIC : *Centre d'Instruction à la Chasse* (Fighter OTU)
CIG : Czechoslovak Inspectorate General
Cz : Czech
(CZ) : Czechoslovak serving in the RAF

CzAF : Cze...
DFC : Distinguished Flying Cross
DFM : Distinguished Flying Medal
DSO : Distinguished Service Order
EC : *Ecole de Chasse* (French), Fighter School
EFTS : Elementary Flying Training School
ELD : *Escadrille Légère de Défense* (French), Fighter Flight
Eva : Evaded
FE : Far East
FIS : Flying Instructors School
F/L : Flight Lieutenant
FLS : Fighter Leaders School
F/O : Flying Officer
FPP : Ferry Pilots Pool
F/Sgt : Flight Sergeant
FTS : Flying Training School
GC : *Groupe de Chasse* (French), Fighter Squadron
GCS : Group Communications Squadron
GSU : Group Support Unit
HQ : Headquarters
HQFC : Headquarters Fighter Command
LAC : Leading Aircraftman
LG : London Gazette
MBE : Member of the Order of the British Empire
ME : Middle East
MU : Maintenance Unit
ORB : Operational Record Book
OTU : Operational Training Unit
(P)AFU : (Pilots) Advanced Flying Unit
PDC : Personnel Despatch Centre
PDRC : Personnel Despatch and Reception Centre
PAF : Polish Air Force
P/O : Pilot Officer
PoW : Prisoner of War
R&SU : Repair and Salvage Unit
SFTS : Service Flying Training School
Sgt : Sergeant
S/L : Squadron Leader
S of AC : School of Army Cooperation
Sqn : Squadron
SS : Signals School
SSC : Short Service Commission
RAF : Royal Air Force
TEU : Tactical Exercice Unit
W/C : Wing Commander
W/O : Warrant Officer

While stationed at Speke during the winter of 1940 - 1941 No.312 (Czech) Squadron was regularly detached to Penrhos. Two Hurricane Mk.Is (V6678/L and P3209/S) can be seen sharing the airfield with Battles and Ansons of No.9 B&GS. (Andrew Thomas)

MAIN EQUIPMENT 1940-1945			
HURRICANE I	08.40 - 05.41	SPITFIRE V	12.41 - 02.44
HURRICANE II	05.41 - 12.41	SPITFIRE VII*	08.43 - 10.43
SPITFIRE II	10.41 - 01.42	SPITFIRE IX	01.44 - 10.45
*Few only			

No.312 (Czechoslovak) Squadron was established as a fighter squadron on 29th August, 1940 by order of the Air Ministry and on 5th September 93 members, including fourteen pilots, of the pre-war Czechoslovakian Air Force gathered at Duxford. They were Pilot Officers Josef Duda, Alois Hlobil, Alois Vasatko, Josef Jaske, Jindrich Bartos, Vlastimil Vesely, Adolf Vrana, Tomas Vybiral, Frantisek Perina and Sgts Josef Keprt, Josef Stehlik, Vaclav Slouf, Jan Truhlar and Frantisek Chabera, and two days later another eleven pilots arrived. The majority of these pilots had gained combat experience in France and had logged between 600 and 2,000 hours.

Flight Lieutenant Dennys E. Gillam took up the position as B Flight's leader on 6th September and Flight Lieutenant Harry A.G. Comerford arrived on 10th September to become the leader of A Flight. Their Czechoslovak deputies were Flight Lieutenants Josef Duda and Alois Hlobil. Squadron Leader Jan Ambrus

arrived two days later, following retraining at No.6 OTU. He was, at this time, the only operational pilot of Slovakian origin serving with the RAF. He had graduated as an observer and was initially posted to *letecky pluk* No.1 (Air Regiment 1) later No.3 and subsequently gained his wings and became a fighter pilot. In 1931-1934 he was appointed as commanding officer of *stihaci letka* No.43 (Fighter Flight 43) of the Air Regiment No.6, and between 1934 and 1939 he became the CO of the Test Flight of Military Technical & Aeronautical Institute .

In March 1939 he was appointed as Commander of the Slovakian Air Force however, following the defection of a number of his pilots to Poland in June, he retired on 1st August, 1939. When Slovakia entered the war he escaped to Belgrade on 3rd September and later joined the Czechoslovakian Air Force in France. Squadron Leader Frank Hastings Tyson was named the Squadron's Commanding Officer on 26th

Serials of Hurricane I in use on 15th October 1940.

L	:	1740, 1748, 1822, 1841, 1807, 1926
P	:	2575, 3268, 3612, 3810, 3888, 3934, 3983
V	:	6542, 6678, 6810, 6811, 6846

Total : 18

September and the unit was issued with Hawker Hurricane Is, some of which had been produced in 1937 and 1938, and these were to cause the Squadron many problems. During September the Squadron lost three Hurricanes due to defective aircraft, however training continued at Duxford until 26th September when the squadron was transferred to Speke, some five miles south-east of Liverpool. They completed their training at this airfield and several pilots also undertook night flying training.

Put into action

No.312 Squadron was now responsible for the defence of Liverpool which had became a target of Luftwaffe night raids. Their first contact with the enemy took place in the afternoon of 8th October 1940. At 1615 hours the standby pilots of Yellow Section began running to their Hurricanes. Flight Lieutenant Dennys E. Gillam and Pilot Officer Alois Vasatko took off immediately but Sergeant Josef Stehlik experienced engine problems and followed them a short time later. Sergeant Stehlik encountered the enemy aircraft at 1,200 feet and it tried to climb into the clouds, however he fired three bursts and the Junkers Ju88 began to descend towards the River Mersey. It was then attacked by D.E. Gillam and A. Vasatko and *Oberleutnant* Helmut Brückmann of KGr 806 was forced to land his burning aircraft on the shore of a bay two and a half miles south-east of Birkenhead. The pilots of Yellow Section returned to base after being airborne for just eleven minutes.

Two days later, on 10th October, the squadron lost its first pilot. At 1339 hours Pilot Officer Bedrich Dvorak and Sergeant Otto Hanzlicek took off on a training flight. After 45 minutes the engine of Hanzlicek´s Hurricane, caught fire and Hanzlicek, a veteran of the fighting in France, baled out but landed in the mud at the mouth of the River Mersey and was drowned. His body was found on 1st November.

During the first weeks of its existence No.312 Squadron was based at Duxford where it took its first Hurricane Is on charge. Behind L1926, already coded DU-J, the newly arrived P2575, formerly of No.73 Squadron can be seen taxiing. This aircraft was subsequently coded DU-P. (Jiri Rajlich)

Another photo taken at Penhros. The Hurricanes had still the under surface of the port wing painted black. In the background is V7686/G. (Andrew Thomas)

THE ORIGINS OF NO.312 SQUADRON'S STORK BADGE

The pilots who formed No.312 Squadron came mainly from two French units, GC I/5 and II/5, which had a stork in their unit insignia.

This tradition can be traced back to WWI when *Escadrille* 67 (left) was created as N 67 in August 1915 (the letter denoted the type of aircraft flown, N being the Nieuport fighter and later SPA stood for SPAD VII and XIII). Its first badge, a flying eagle superimposed on a light and dark brown triangle, was a reminder of capitaine de Saint-Sauveur's (its first C/O) horse racing colours.

Renamed SPA 67, when it converted to SPAD VIIs at the end of 1917, the unit was integrated into the famous "*Groupe des Cigognes*" (Stork Wing) under *capitaine* Brocard. At the same time, the eagle was replaced by a stork. Escadrille 67 claimed 42 confirmed victories and had four aces, not including the famous Jean Navarre who served for just a short spell.

It became 1st *escadrille* of GC I/5 at Lyons in 1932, the designation it still retained on the eve of WWII. Between the two wars it flew various types of fighters and, under the command of *capitaine* J-M. Accart it was converted to Curtiss H-75As in the summer of 1939. Accart met Frantisek Perina at the international Meeting held in Zurich in 1937 and, having appreciated his flying skills, he managed to have him transferred to his escadrille just after the outbreak of WWII.

SPA 167 (right) was formed in August 1918, under *capitaine* du Barny de Romanet, and earmarked to become the fifth fighter unit of GC 12, the "*Groupe des Cigognes*", hence its badge. It took no part in the fighting before October but claimed 17 confirmed victories in less than a month. Eight of them were credited to Romanet and brought his grand total up to 18. Disbanded in April 1919, it was reformed in 1921 and became 4th *escadrille* of GC II/5 at Lyons in 1932. The unit converted to Curtiss H-75As a few months before Germany invaded Poland.

Next day at 1750 hours two sections of Hurricanes, Yellow Section led by Flight Lieutenant H.A.G. Comerford and Red Section by Squadron Leader F.H. Tyson, along with two sections of Spitfires of No.611 Squadron, took off to intercept enemy bombers. Shortly after they were airborne Pilot Officer Alois Vasatko and Sergeant Josef Keprt, the wing men of Yellow Section, lost sight of their leader and joined up with Red Section.

Harry Comerford, now flying alone spotted a Dornier Do17Z and he attacked three times but without visible success. At 1825 hours the five Hurricanes patrolling between Prestatyn and Chester spotted a Do17 at a height of 21,000 feet and continuously attacked it until they ran out of ammunition, however the enemy aircraft, with one engine burning, still managed to escape but subsequently crashed into Caernarvon Bay. No.312 Squadron's pilots returned to Speke between 1840 and 1850 hours by which time fog was enveloping the airfield only to find that the victory had been awarded to Flight Lieutenant W.J. Leather, Pilot Officers P.S.C. Pollard and J.R.G. Sutton of No.611 Squadron who had also attacked it.

Two days a section led by Squadron Leader Jan Ambrus took off at 1750 hours to investigate a contact believed to be enemy bombers. The section climbed to 11,000 feet and the pilots spotted two twin engined bombers 4,000 feet below them and, confident that these were Ju88s, they attacked. It was a bitter mistake as the aircraft which Squadron Leader Ambrus, Flight Lieutenant Harry Comerford and Sergeant Stehlik shot down was a Bristol Blenheim IF of No.29 Squadron being flown by Sergeant R.E. Stevens. Fortunately the second aircraft, flown by Pilot Officer J.D. Humphreys, was only damaged and he managed to land it at Ternhill.

On 15th October a section led by Squadron Leader Ambrus took off on a patrol at 1730 hours, however due to heavy rain the pilots became disorientated and unable to see the ground. They continued flying until they ran out of fuel. Flight Lieutenant H. Comerford and Pilot Officer Tomas Vybiral, baled out however Ambrus managed to belly land north of Lancaster at 2015 hours.

TOWARDS THE END OF THE BATTLE OF BRITAIN

Luftwaffe day activity over Liverpool was minimal as it was too far for escorting fighters to accompany the bombers and No.312 Squadron did not see much combat. Meanwhile the pilots perfected their night flying skills. During the last two last months of 1940 there were a number of changes in the command structure. Flight Lieutenant Charles A. Cooke was

Winter 1940 -1941 was harsh with low temperatures and snow, nevertheless operations had to continue. P3612/N is seen here awaiting its pilot. This aircraft was wrecked a couple of weeks later by Sergeant F. Kruta. (Jiri Rajlich)

posted in from No.66 Squadron on 18th November to take over A Flight and two days later the Czechoslovakian flight commanders, Flight Lieutenants Josef Duda and Alois Hlobil, were posted to No.4 Ferry Pilots Pool Headquarters. They were succeeded by Flight Lieutenants Jan Klan and Alois Vasatko, both of whom had become aces in the Battle of France. On 1st December Flight Lieutenant Dennys E. Gillam, the leader of B Flight, left the squadron to become the Commanding Officer of No.306 (Polish) Squadron and he was replaced by Flight Lieutenant A.M. Dawbarn from that squadron. On 12th December the 41 year old Czechoslovak commanding officer Jan Ambrus was succeeded by 36 year old Squadron Leader Evzen Cizek who was posted in from No.1 Squadron. But, in another hand, if the British pilots were leaving, giving place to Czech pilots, half of the ground crew was still British.

Late on the 29th of November a section of three Hurricanes caught up with a Dornier Do215 at a height of 21,000 ft. Only Sergeant Josef Keprt managed to inflict damage on the aircraft and he reported that he had hit the gunner and had seen the port engine trailing smoke.

B Flight was detached to Penrhos Airfield in Caernavonshire on 21st and 22nd December, 1940 and from this base it carried out combat patrols over St George's Channel until 20th April 1941. There were few opportunities for combat with Luftwaffe planes

over the west coast of England so some of the pilots who had night flying experience were posted to No.96 Squadron at their own request. On 8th February Pilot Officer Vlastimil Vesely and Pilot Officer Josef Kloboucnik were posted out of the Squadron and on 24th March they were followed by Pilot Officer Josef Keprt and Flight Sergeant Frantisek Chabera.

On 13th February 1941, Flying Officer Jindrich Bartos, a veteran of the Battle of France was killed in a training accident when his Hurricane, spun in at Talacre north-east of Prestatyn. Sergeant Frantisek Kruta was luckier when he crashed during take off on 22nd February as his Hurricane, was destroyed but he was only slightly injured. A further incident occurred on 1st March when Flying Officer Tomas Kruml made a belly landing at Penrhos. The Squadron headquarters and A Flight were transferred to Valley on 3rd March to carry out patrols over the Irish Sea, however both flights were to be reunited at Jurby on the Isle of Man on 20th April.

After more than five months No.312 Squadron finally gained a confirmed victory. On the morning of 14th March Green Section, led by Flight Lieutenant A. Dawbarn, attacked a reconnaissance Ju88. Dawbarn attacked, followed by Sergeant J. Stehlik who fired from a range of 100 yards and the German aircraft, crashed into the sea 25 miles south-west of Bardsey Island. But accidents were again recorded as four days later Flying Officer Jan Cermak made a belly landing near Dolgarrog and on 6th April Sergeant Stehlik, the

squadron's most successful pilot, had to make a forced landing on a beach.

Squadron Leader Frank H. Tyson, the British commanding officer, left the squadron on 1st April and B Flight lost its leader on 10th April. Flight Lieutenant A.M. Dawbarn took off on a combat patrol with Sgt Jan Truhlar and at 1435 hours they attacked a twin engine aircraft. It was subsequently credited as damaged but Dawbarn failed to return. It is possible that he was hit by return fire and crashed, unobserved, into the sea.

On 20th April both flights were posted to Jurby on the Isle of Man, an island which is best known for the Tourist Trophy motorcycle races, to replace No.258 Squadron and the Czechoslovak squadron carried out day and night patrols over the Irish Sea until 16th May. Flight Sergeant Bohumil Votruba was killed during a night training flight on 6th May when the weather turned bad and he decided to land in England but had to bale out. His body was found next day at Loweswater in Cumberland.

Fligh Lieutenant Jan Cermak left the squadron on 19th May to take up an appointment as the Czechoslovak leader of No.313 (Czech) Squadron's B Flight, this unit being the last Czech fighter Squadron to be formed during the war. Soon afterwards Flight Lieutenant Josef Jaske was named the Czechoslovak commander of No.313 Squadron and he took up his new appointment on 21st July 1941. On this day Flight Lieutenant Jan Cermak returned

to lead No.312 Squadron's A Flight.

Their stay on the Isle of Man was approaching an end and on 27th May Squadron Leader Jan Klan, another veteran of the fighting in France, succeeded Squadron Leader Evzen Cizek. A day later Flight Lieutenant Charles A Cooke, A Flight's leader, departed from the squadron and it now consisted solely of Czechoslovak pilots.

NEW PLANES FOR THE CZECHS

On 29th May the squadron joined the Kenley Wing, was re-equipped with Hurricane Mk.IIs and began attacking targets in France and Belgium. Klan led the Squadron for a only short time before being replaced on 5th June by Squadron Leader Alois Vasatko, one of the best fighter aces of the Battle of France, who till this time had led B Flight. The new commander of B Flight was Flight Lieutenant Tomas Vybiral, another veteran of the the fighting in the French Campaign.

On 14th June 1941, No.312 Squadron took part in *Circus* 12. The target was the airfield at St. Omer-Fort Rouge and the Wing, comprising Nos.1, 303 and 312 Squadrons escorted twelve Bristol Blenheims of No.110 Squadron to the target. The Czechoslovak squadron encountered no enemy aircraft and returned, without loss, to their base.

They again caught up with the Luftwaffe at 1730 hours on 18th June when the Kenley Wing, now

Hurricane I V7066/DU-T arrived at the squadron on 18.12.40, and was lost some four months later, on 10.04.41, while being flown by Flight Lieutenant A.A.M. Dawbarn, who became the only British pilot killed while serving with No.312 Squadron. (Jiri Rajlich)

FIGHTER COMMAND

After experiencing Zeppelin and bomber attacks during the First World War, Britons were well aware that they were vulnerable from the air and the German re-armament programme of the thirties did nothing but further increase this fear. Despite an enlargement process Fighter Command could only boast 25 regular squadrons, two from the special reserve and 12 Auxiliary squadrons when war fell in September 1939. Not only was this number well short of the 57 squadrons deemed necessary for the Air Defence of Great Britain but, of the existing 39, not all were fully operational.

During the first year of the war Fighter Command was expanded somewhat and at the successful conclusion of the Battle of Britain, which would be it's greatest achievement, had almost 70 squadrons on its Battle Order. When the planning for the Invasion of Europe commenced squadrons were divided into defensive and offensive roles and Fighter Command disappeared on 15th November 1943. It was superseded by Air Defence of Great Britain (ADGB), which was responsible for the defence of the British Isles, and the 2nd Tactical Air Force, which was in charge of the offensive actions.

At the split-up Fighter Command had approximately 100 squadrons under its umbrella but this was reduced by a third with the inception of the 2nd TAF, which would become the RAF's spearhead for the Invasion. In October 1944 when the advance of Allied troops appeared irreversible, and the Luftwaffe's effort was concentrated mainly on the Eastern front, ADGB re-adopted its original name of Fighter Command. However its needs were not what they had once been and at the German surrender barely 40 squadrons remained under its control.

From its inception Fighter Command was organised into Groups, with geographical boundaries, which would vary in accordance with the changing circumstances of the time. Originally just three Groups, No's 11, 12 and 13 were responsible for the defence of the whole of British Isles, but resources were too thinly spread and by the end of 1940, another three had been re-activated.

Chronologically the Groups were:

<u>No.11 Group</u>: Reformed at Uxbridge on 1st May 1936, it fell under the control of Fighter Command on 14th July. This Group was responsible for the South and, later, the Southeast region of England, which included London. During the Battle of Britain it was situated closest to the enemy and controlled the largest number of squadrons. It went onto the offensive when Fighter Command began attacks across the English Channel in 1941.

<u>No.12 Group</u>: Reformed at Hucknall on 1st April 1937 and was immediately placed under Fighter Command control to defend the central area of England. This included protecting the region located immediately north of No.11 Group, and the Midland industrial area, including the east and west parts south of the Humber.

<u>No.13 Group</u>: Reformed at Newcastle on 15th March 1939 and immediately placed under the control of Fighter Command to ease the pressure on No.12 Group. Its zone initially comprised industrial areas north of the Humber and southern Scotland.

<u>No.10 Group</u>: Reformed at Rudloe Manor on 1st June 1940 primarily to cover the Southwest of England and protect shipping in the western half of the channel. It was absorbed into No.11 Group on 2nd May 1945.

<u>No.14 Group</u>: Reformed at Inverness on 29th June 1940 to protect Scotland. It was absorbed into No.13 Group on 15th July 1943.

<u>No.9 Group</u>: Reformed at Preston on 9th August 1940 to protect the north-west of England and Northern Ireland. It was absorbed into No.12 Group on 15th September 1944.

consisting of Nos.1, 258 and 312 Squadrons, was providing the close escort for six Blenheims of No.107 Squadron. On their way back from a raid on Bois de Liques they were bounced by Bf109s. Sergeant Otmar Kucera came under attack but managed to break away and got into position on the tail of one of the three attackers. He fired two bursts at a Bf109 and the first hit the left wing and the second the cockpit but as no one saw the Bf109 crash it was only credited with a probably destroyed. Sergeant Josef Stehlik also manage to damage a Bf109.

No.312 Squadron's next operation was *Circus* 17, on the afternoon of 21st June, when they escorted six Blenheims to Desvres airfield but once again they failed to meet up with the Luftwaffe. Two days later the squadron escorted Blenheims to the power station at Chocques, near Bethune however shortly after take off the Hurricanes piloted by Flying Officer Tomas Kruml and Sergeant Jozef Mensik collided. Josef Mensik managed to make an emergency landing near Maidstone however T. Kruml, had to bale out. The squadron returned to the fray on 27th June as part of *Circus* 25 and escorted 22 Blenheims on a raid on the steel works in Lille.

During formation flying training on 29th June the squadron lost two Hurricanes, when Flight Lieutenant Tomas Vybiral and Pilot Officer Svatopluk Bachurek collided. Both pilots survived but S. Bachurek had to make an emergency landing and T. Vybiral baled out. The squadron gained its next confirmed victory on 3rd July 1941 when the Kenley Wing escorted six Blenheims of No.18 Squadron to the marshalling yard at Hazebrouck. Over the target the Blenheims were attacked by ten Bf109Fs and Sergeant Otmar Kucera got one of them in his gun sight and fired two bursts. The Bf109 went into a spin and the pilot baled out.

During *Circus* 33 they escorted four Stirlings to the steel works in Lille, and Flight Sergeant Vojtech Smolik scored hits on one of the five Bf109 which intercepted the formation and this was credited as a probable. The squadron was again in action on 8th July when the Kenley Wing escorted *Circus* 39, three Stirlings, to bomb Lens. At 0630 hours the British formation was attacked by four groups of fighters from JG 26 and JG 2 and the Czechoslovak squadron claimed one confirmed and one damaged but lost Sergeant Jozef Mensik, who managed avoid capture. "*Jozo*" Mensik travelled across France, over the Pyrenees and, after a period of detention in the camp at Miranda, he reached Gibraltar on 1st October and was back in Britain three weeks later. In this action the Squadron´s score was increased by Flight Sergeant Vojtech Smolik who gained a confirmed victory over a Bf109 and Josef Stehlik who claimed one Bf109 damaged.

The following afternoon the Stirlings attacking

Hurricane IIB Z3588 in June 1941. The squadron code "DU" is now positioned behind the roundel. (Jiri Rajlich)

CODENAMES - OFFENSIVE OPERATIONS

CIRCUS :
Bombers heavily escorted by fighters, the purpose being to bring enemy fighters into combat.

RAMROD :
Bombers escorted by fighters, the primary aim being to destroy a target.

RANGER :
Large formation freelance intrusion over enemy territory with aim of wearing down enemy figthers.

RHUBARD :
Freelance fighter sortie against targets of opportunity.

ROADSTEAD :
Low level attack on coastal shipping

RODEO :
A fighter sweep without bombers.

SWEEP :
An offensive flight by fighters designed to draw up and clear the enemy from the sky.

Bethune and No.312 Squadron again supplied the escort. About an hour into the operation the formation came into contact with Bf109Fs of JG 2 and JG 26 and Sergeant Antonin Zavoral scored first at 1359 hours when he shot down a Bf109 between Hucqeliers and Fruges. Moments later Squadron Leader Vasatko damaged another and then at 1412 he got a second one which was credited as a probable. Flight Sergeant Otmar Kucera also destroyed one Bf109 however the squadron lost two aircraft. Flight Sergeant Ladislav Svetlik landed his damaged aircraft in England but Fligh Sergeant Jan Truhlar had to bale out of his Hurricane over France and became a PoW. He was, in all probability, shot down by *Leutnant* Erich Rudorffer of 6./JG 2.

On 10th July, during *Circus* 42, the Kenley Wing escorted three Stirlings to Chocques. In cloudy conditions they were intercepted on their way home and in fierce combat four of the Wing's Spitfires were shot down, however the Czechoslovak squadron returned without loss. Flight Sergeant J. Stehlik managed to score hits on one Bf109 which was credited as a probable. This was the squadron's last combat while it was part of the Kenley Wing. The squadron was transferred to Martlesham Heath, east of Ipswich, on July 20th where it replaced No.310 (Czech) Squadron and Flight Lieutenant Josef Jaske, A Flight's leader, was posted out of the squadron on the same day.

The squadron now carried out convoy patrols and, while the pilots recognised the importance of such operations, they considered it boring. During this relatively quiet period Squadron Leader T. Vasatko came up with the idea of forming of a purely Czechoslovak fighter wing. In the middle of August he sent his suggestion to his superior at the Inspectorate of Czechoslovak Air Force in London and in May 1942, the Czechoslovak Wing became a reality.

No.312 Squadron was posted north to Scotland on 19th

SERIALS OF HURRICANE IIB IN USE ON 1ST SEPTEMBER 1941.

Z : 2987, 2988, 3021, 3181, 3221, 3242, 3323, 3437, 3501, 3588, 3592, 3660, 3742, 4994, 5060
AP : 519

Total : 16

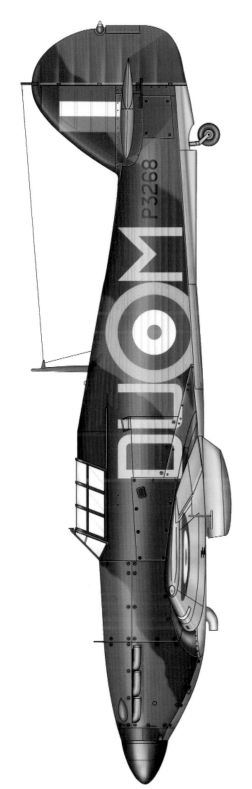

Hawker Hurricane Mk.I P3268, No.312 (Czechoslovak) Squadron, Flight Lieutenant D. E. Gillam (RAF), Speke, October 1940.
Note the absence of any Czech roundel.
Was it because it was the mount of a British pilot, or because it was not painted yet, it is not unclear.

One of the first Hurricane IIAs, Z2836, to be used by No.312 Squadron in June 1941. This aircraft is being taxied by Sergeant M. Standera. (Andrew Thomas)

THE HAWKER **HURRICANE**

The Hawker Hurricane was the first of the RAF's monoplane fighters and the prototype flew for the first time on 6th November 1935.

The initial version, powered by a Merlin II of 1,030 hp, was designated the **Hurricane Mk.I** and was ordered in quantity during the summer of 1936 to rearm the RAF's fighter squadrons. The first aircraft were delivered during the Autumn of 1937 and the type became operational in January 1938. On the eve of the Second World War, nearly 500 Hurricanes had been delivered to the RAF and they were the backbone of Fighter Command until late 1940.

After the Battle of Britain, the Hurricane gave way to the Spitfire as the main fighter of Fighter Command, as squadrons were gradually re-equipped.

It was at that time that the **Hurricane M.II**, with the more powerful Merlin XX of 1,390 hp engine appeared, but its performance remained inferior to that of German fighters, and the Hurricane seemed to have reached its limit of development. Because of this the Hurricane I and II would remain the two main production versions.

From mid-1941, the Hurricane was used, briefly, as a night fighter and with more success as a fighter-bomber. Considerable numbers were shipped to other theatres of operations for service in this role however it gradually disappeared from combat in Europe as the RAF introduced new types into service.

However the Hurricane remained in first line service until the end of the war in the Mediterranean, and in the Far East, after which it quickly disappeared from the RAF inventory.

August 1941 and the pilots flew nineteen Hurricane IIs to their new base at Ayr by way of a refuelling stop at Leconfield. The rest of the personnel travelled by train or on board Bristol Bombay transports. On 20th September 1941 Air Vice Marshall Karel Janousek visited the squadron on the occasion of the first anniversary of its formation. One month later the squadron received its first six Supermarine Spitfire IIAs and several days later began training on this new type of fighter. The squadron lost its first Spitfire on 25th October during a training flight when Flying Officer Frantisek Hekl brushed a wing against the surface of Loch Doon. The wing broke off the aircraft disappeared into the loch taking the pilot with it. The rescue action was unsuccessful and the aircraft was not located until the summer of 1982.

The visit of President Edvard Benes, of the Czechoslovak Republic, on 13th November curtailed the normal activities of the squadron on that day. Of greater significance perhaps was the re-equipment of

Hurricane IIB Z3242 in June 1941. By Summer 1941 Fighter Command was back on the offensive over Europe and Hurricanes still equipped half of the single-engined squadrons involved in day operations. (Jiri Rajlich)

the Squadron with Spitfire VBs at the end of November.

During combat training on 19ᵗʰ December the Spitfires flown by Sergeant Jaroslav Kucera and Flight Sergeant Vojtech Smolik collided. Vojtech Smolik managed to bale out but Kucera crashed in the vicinity of Newmilus and was killed. Conversion to Spitfire Mk.Vs was soon accomplished and on New Years Day 1942 the squadron moved to its new base at Fairwood Common in Glamorganshire. It shared this base with No.615 Squadron but remained attached to No.10 Group. Late in January it was posted to Angle in Pembrokeshire and the unit spent nearly three months there.

The Squadron's first Spitfire kill was achieved by Pilot Officer Otmar Kucera on the morning of 16ᵗʰ February 1942 when, during a convoy patrol, he shot down a Ju88 near Linney Head. In the afternoon of 21ˢᵗ March Red Section, led by Flight Lieutenant Bedrich Dvorak, took off to intercept a suspected bandit. When they spotted the Ju88 he and Sergeant Jaroslav Dobrovolny fired on the enemy aircraft but even with two engines on fire it managed to escape. Both pilots were given credit for a half probable. During the attacks the enemy gunner scored hits on Dobrovolny's Spitfire and his

right leg was injured. The aircraft was damaged when he landed and did not become operational until May. In the meantime the squadron had moved back to Fairwood Common on 18ᵗʰ April.

CZECHOSLOVAK WING

Its next move was to Harrowbeer, a satellite airfield in the Exeter Sector, on 3ʳᵈ May where the squadron replaced No.302 (Polish) Squadron and became part of the newly established Czechoslovak Wing comprising Nos.310, 312 and 154 Squadrons. Wing Commander Alois Vasatko, hitherto the commanding officer of No.312 Squadron, was appointed as its commanding officer and Squadron Leader Jan Cermak, who had led A Flight was put in command of the Squadron. The Wing came under the control of the Exeter Sector on 7ᵗʰ May and during its early days as a Wing it practised formation flying.

On the morning of 29ᵗʰ May the Wing took off from the airfields at Exeter, Harrowbeer and Church Stanton and flew over to Warmwell. After refuelling they took off at 1105 hours to meet up with the Ibsley Wing to participate in *Rodeo* 11 but the weather turned bad and the raid on Le Havre Harbour was can-

Like many fighter squadron No.312 Squadron began to be re-equipped with Spitfires in 1941 - 1942. Having flown Spitfire IIAs for just a few weeks the Czech pilots received Spifire Vs which were the best RAF fighters at that time. Spitfire VB AD553/DU-E (illustrated) was lost along with its pilot, Flight Lieutenant R. Rohacek, on 27.04.42. (Andrew Thomas).

celled. On 1st June No.312 Squadron took off on what was hoped to be the first real action involving the Czechoslovak Wing however no enemy aircraft were seen during *Rodeo* 12, but two days later everything changed.

On the morning of 3rd June the Squadron again flew over to Warmwell where it joined the other squadrons of the Wing. Under the leadership of Flight Lieutenant Tomas Vybiral it took off at 1440 hours to escort *Circus* 6, six Bostons of No.107 Squadron, on a raid on Cherbourg. Forty-five minutes into the operation FW190s avoided No.310 (Czech) Squadron, which was flying as top cover, and attacked No.312 Squadron. In the melee which followed JG 2 claimed 14 victories without any losses and No.312 Squadron claimed one FW190 as destroyed, one probable victory and four FW190s as damaged.

The most successful pilot was Flying Officer Frantisek Perina, a veteran of the Battle in France, who had gained 11 confirmed victories while serving with *Groupe de Chasse* I/5. He shot down one FW190 and damaged another. One FW190 was credited to Flying Officer Ivo Tonder as probably destroyed, before he was in turn shot down. Ivo Tonder's Spitfire crashed into the Channel and he became a PoW after being picked up by a Heinkel He59. Pilot Officer

Karel Posta damaged two FW190s, Flight Lieutenant Antonin Liska damaged one however Flight Lieutenant Bedrich Dvorak, and Sergeant D.J. King of No.154 Squadron also became prisoners of war. Flight Lieutenant B. Dvorak was rescued by French fishermen who had to hand him over to the Germans. Two days later the Squadron took off on *Circus* 7 to escort a dozen Bostons to Morlaix airfield. After the bombardment the RAF formation was attacked by eight FW190s of III./JG 2. The squadron, which flew as top cover didn´t take part in this skirmish, however on 6th June the squadron covered the return of Hurricanes which had attacked targets near St. Valery. On 8th June No.154 Squadron left the wing and was replaced at Church Stanton by No.313 (Czechoslovak) Squadron from the Hornchurch Wing. The Wing's next operation was a raid on the airfield at Lannion with all three Czechoslovak fighter squadrons participating. The squadron was transferred from Harrowbeer to Bold Head on the morning of 10th June and after the short briefing it again took off again at 0840 hours to escort twelve of No.107 Squadron's Bostons. However the bombers took too long to get into formation and the Wing Commander cancelled the operation. At 1300 hours the order was given for a new start and twenty minutes later the escort met up with the Bostons over Cape Start Point. Fighters from III./JG 2 intercepted the raid however the Czechoslovak Wing returned without loss although one Boston was shot down. For the next few days the squadron returned to convoy escort duties.

At 1820 hours on 23rd June twelve Spitfires of No.312 Squadron, along with a dozen Spitfires each from of Nos.310 and No.313 Squadrons, took off from Exeter. The Wing formed up at 1830 hours and No.312 Squadron flew as top cover for six Bostons going to bomb Morlaix airfield. The Wing was led by Wing Commander Alois Vasatko, No.312 Squadron's former commanding officer, and at 1905 hours the airfield was attacked and the formation turned towards the French coast. It was followed by FW190s which were initially driven off, however near Cape Start Point ten FW190s of 7./JG 2 led by *Oberleutnant* Egon Mayer again attacked the formation.

Alois Vasatko ordered his fighters to break formation and pulled his Spitfire into an ascending turn and struck the FW190A-3 flown by *Unteroffizier* Wilhelm Reuschling. Both fighters crashed into the Channel. Wing Commander A. Vasatko died but the German was rescued by the crew of an ASR boat and became a PoW. Flight Lieutenant Karel Kasal was hit in the right leg but despite this he managed to land at Exeter and his ground crew got him out of the cockpit. The aircraft of Flight Sergeant Vaclav Ruprecht and Flying Officer Frantisek Perina were also slightly damaged

while landing. Their next loss was Fligh Sergeant Frantisek Mares, who collided with a No.310 Squadron Spitfire flown by Pilot Officer Jaromir Strihavka when the alert section took off from Bold Head.

On 29th June, at 1332 hours, Flight Lieutenant Antonin Liska and Sergeant Stanislav Tocauer took off to intercept a reconnaissance aircraft. The leader climbed to a height of 32,000 feet and dived on the German. At that moment both wings of his Spitfire collapsed and it crashed on the beach near Sidmouth at 1415 hours. The pilot survived the horrific crash despite receiving multiple injuries.

Despite being mostly employed on convoy patrols at this time the squadron had the opportunity of putting things right on 12th July. At 1230 hours Warrant Officer Jaroslav Sodek and Sergeant Josef Novotny took off from Harrowbeer to escort a convoy. Thirty minutes into the patrol they received warning of an enemy aircraft in the area and this proved to be a Ju88. Jaroslav Sodek fired three bursts silencing the gunner and then fired the rest of his ammunition into the fuselage and cockpit but the aircraft did not go down. This was credited as damaged.

The action continued on 30th July when the Squadron escorted Hurricanes on two coastal shipping strikes. The first was to Les Sept Isles which was followed by one to Batz Island. The next day they provided cover for twelve Bostons raiding the docks in St.

Spitfire VB BL381 just before it was damaged by Sergeant Jaroslav Dobrovolny on 21.03.42. (Jiri Rajlich)

Spitfires of No.312 Squadron taxying out for another sortie during Operation *Jubilee* on 19.08.42. The squadron flew three missions that day, claiming two confirmed victories, one being shared, two probables and three aircraft damaged. Additionally an armed boat was destroyed. (Andrew Thomas)

Malô harbour. No.312 Squadron flew over the continent on 5th August when the Exeter (Czechoslovak) Wing took part in *Rodeo* 15 a patrol over Cherbourg. Next day, together with No.310 Squadron, they escorted ten Hurricanes to attack shipping near Les Sept Isles.

Operations in August culminated on the 19th during Operation *Jubilee*. However before this, on 17th August the whole Wing took part in *Circus* 204, a sweep over Cherbourg. The purpose of this *Circus* was to draw the attention of Luftwaffe fighters away from eighteen B-17Es of 97th BG while they bombed the marshalling yard at Rouen-Sotteville but the ruse was unsuccessful and the Czechoslovak squadrons did not see any enemy aircraft.

This was the first mission to be flown by bombers of the USAAF's 8th Air Force and was led by the Group Commander, Colonel Frank Armstrong. Brigadier General Ira Eaker, the chief of the VIII Bomber Command, also took part in this attack. Following this mission the Squadron, together with No.310 Squadron, moved to Redhill and on the next day both Czechoslovak squadrons, and No.350 (Belgian) Squadron, under the command of Wing Commander Karel Mrazek, carried out a combat patrol around Abbeville, Le Trépot and Berck-sur-Mer but the Abbeville Boys failed to respond.

THE CZECHS OVER DIEPPE

That evening they were given advanced warning of an operation which would take place early next morning. They were woken up early and the two Czechoslovak squadrons, led by Wing Commander K. Mrazek, took off at 0755 hours to escort the Hurricanes of Nos.3 and 43 Squadrons to attack E-boats reportedly sailing from Boulogne to Dieppe. Squadron Leader Jan Cermak led No.312 Squadron however the E-boats could not be found so the attackers were redirected to Boulogne where they were welcomed by heavy *flak* which shot down one of the Hurricanes.

They then flew to Dieppe and encountered some armed barges and Flight Sergeant Josef Pipa damaged one of them, however no E-boats could be found and No.312 Squadron landed back at Redhill at 0935 hours. Its Spitfires were re-fuelled and re-armed and at 1050 hours twelve of the squadron's aircraft again took off and, together with No.416 (RCAF) and No.616 Squadrons, flew over Dieppe.

The thirty six Spitfires led by Wing Commander Duke-Woolley arrived at 1115 hours and patrolled in sections of four aircraft with the Czechs flying at heights of between 4500 and 6650 feet. A quarter of an hour later FW190s attacked from 2 O'clock high and in the subsequent combat No.312 Squadron claimed two FW190s as probables and two damaged. Flight

Hawker Hurricane Mk.I V6678, No.312 (Czechoslovak) Squadron, Pilot Officer A. Vrana, Penrhos, December 1940. Of the three Czechoslovakian fighter squadrons, No.312 Squadron was the one where the CzAF insignia was regulary painted beneath the cockpit of its aircraft.

Re-arming the aircraft. In every operational squadron the ground crews played an important role in keeping the unit at peak efficiency. (Andrew Thomas)

Sergeant Vaclav Ruprecht, of Yellow Section, was credited with one probable while Pilot Officer Vojtech Smolik damaged another one. Sergeant Miroslav Liskutin, another member of Yellow Section, damaged a FW190 but his Spitfire was in turn heavily damaged. He managed to bring his aircraft home despite a 28 inch hole in the right wing. This was the sole combat damaged inflicted on the squadron during Operation *Jubilee*. Sergeant Tomas Motycka, who flew as Number 2 to the squadron commander, was credited with a second probable. The Squadron returned to base at 1245 hours.

While the pilots ate lunch the aircraft were refuelled and re-armed and at 1410 hours No.312 Squadron, led by Squadron Leader Jan Cermak, took off on the last operation of the day. It patrolled over a convoy for nearly an hour when a group of unescorted Do217s was sighted. The squadron attacked the bombers and Flight Lieutenant Karel Kasal, B Flight's leader, closed to within 50 yards of one bomber but when he tried to fire his guns he found that his guns were not adjusted. His Number 2, Flight Sergeant Josef Pipa, damaged one Do217 and Flying Officer Josef Keprt shot down another bomber in a frontal attack. Sergeant M. Liskutin shared a kill with a pilot of No.131 squadron. The Squadron landed back at its

---

SERIALS OF SPITFIRE V IN USE ON 1ST JANUARY 1942.

R :	6833 (Mk.VA)		**W** :	3249, 3445
AA :	970		**AB** :	172
AD :	415, 541, 553, 572			
BL :	252, 254, 260, 289, 343, 381, 487, 512, 516, 529			

Total : 19

Two Spitfires Mk.IIs were also on charge, P8347 and P8570.

base at 1610 hours and the next morning it returned to Harrowbeer where they reverted to convoy patrols, alert standbys against fighter-bomber raids and escorts over the Channel and the Continent.

Flight Lieutenant Karel Kasal was posted out on 25th August and his successor was Flight Lieutenant Adolf Vrana a veteran of *Groupe de Chasse* I/5 who had fought in the Battle of France.

On 31st August the squadron escorted three Westland Whirlwinds to attack shipping near the island of Jersey and on 4th September at 1851 hours the standby section, Flight Sergeant Josef Pipa and Flight Sergeant Miroslav Liskutin took off against six fighter-bombers FW190s of 10 (Jabo)./JG 2 which had attacked targets in Torquay. The two men made visual contact with four of the raiders and pursued them across the Channel however they could not catch them.

Four days later No.312 Squadron together with No.310 Squadron escorted six Bostons returning from a raid on Cherbourg and on 10th September they, and No.310 Squadron, covered the return of four Whirlwinds from the island of Jersey. The Wing took part in *Circus* 10, an attack on the "Solglint" in Cherbourg Harbour on 15th September. Flight Lieutenant Karel Kasal took over B Flight on 29th September.

Two days later, *Roadstead* 36, consisting of four Whirlwinds escorted by the squadron, attacked ships in the port of Lezardrieux and on 9th October the squadron patrolled over Rotterdam as part of *Circus* 224. Next day No.312 Squadron was transferred to Church Stanton where it was based alongside No.313 (Czech) Squadron.

NEW ACTIVITIES

With the arrival of the USAAF's 8th Air Force in the United Kingdom the RAF's activities were extended to providing escorts for the American bombers as they did not, as yet, have any of their own fighters in the theatre. It was for this reason that No.312 Squadron was called upon to escort American bombers on their attacks on the Kriegsmarine's U-Boat bases. The first such operation took place on 21st October 1942 when the squadron flew as rear cover for 66 Boeing B-17s and 24 Consolidated B-24s attacking the Lorient base. Five days later the squadron performed two *Rhubarbs*, 92 and 93, between Morlaix and Guingamp. Next day another *Rhubarb* was carried out in the same area and later the same day the Wing was sent to patrol over Cherbourg. Eight Hurricanes were escorted to attack shipping in Lorient harbour on 28th October.

On 7th November the Squadron escorted two American raids. At noon 23 B-17s of 91st and 306th BG bombed Brest and at 1600 hours a dozen B-24s struck the same target without incident. During *Ramrod* 36, an escort for B-24s of 93rd BG, the Wing arrived late and only caught up with the bombers over the target. After hitting the target the bombers turned for home and the Czechoslovak Wing took up position to defend the formation. This manoeuvre brought the fighters to within 500 yards of the bombers and the nervous gunners opened fire on the "unknown" aircraft to their rear. At this point Flight Sergeant Stanislav Tocauer of No.312 Squadron was attacked by two FW190s and Flight Sergeant M. Liskutin fired at the two enemy aircraft but they

A trio of Spitfire VBs and VCs at Harrowbeer in September 1942. In front is AR511/DU-U with EP660/DU-O and EP564/DU-E on its right. (Andrew Thomas)

escaped by diving. The American gunners stopped firing at the Czechoslovak's aircraft escort, however when the Squadron returned to base it was found that Pilot Officer Vaclav Slouf had five 0.5 inch bullet holes in his aircraft. The American apologised for this incident. It became the last event of the year.

Flight Lieutenant Kasal, B Flight leader, was posted out of the Squadron soon after and was succeeded by Flight Lieutenant Tomas Vybiral who was promoted to the rank of Squadron Leader and on 1st January 1943 he took command of the Squadron.

On 6th January Flight Sergeant Miroslav Liskutin crashed while landing and his Spitfire, which was written off. On the 15th January, No.312 Squadron, along with the other squadrons of Exeter Wing, took part in *Circus* 13. At the end of the month, the Wing was once again escorting bombers to targets in France, participating to *Ramrod* 47, 48, 49 and 50 between 21st and 29th January 1943.

Escorting bombers continued throughout February and March and while the Wing lost several pilots No.312 Squadron returned without losses but regrettably without scoring any victories. On 1st February 1943 Flight Lieutenant Viktor Kaslik, A Flight's leader was succeeded by Flight Lieutenant Karel Kasal and on 20th February the Squadron was transferred to Warmwell. After several days, on 6th March, it came back to Church Stanton.

The Squadron's first success in 1943 was gained on 4th April when, under the command of Wing Comamnder Frantisek Dolezal, the new commander of the Wing, twenty-two Spitfires of Nos.312 and 313 squadrons escorted a dozen Venturas of No.464 (RAAF) Squadron on *Ramrod* 62 to the marshalling yard in St. Briene. At 1545 hours the formation was attacked by FW190s of III./JG 2 and Flight Sergeant Stanislav Tocauer fired a five seconds burst, from 400 yards, at one of the attackers and this was claimed as a probable.

The first pilot lost in 1943 was Flying Officer Jaroslav Novak who was killed on 14th May when at 2030 hours No.312 Squadron, together with No.313 Squadron ran into heavy *flak* while attacking shipping at St Peter Port on the island of Guernsey. The first Spitfire to be hit was the Spitfire flown by Squadron Leader Vybiral but he managed return to base. Novak's Spitfire received a hit direct in the engine, he attempted to land on the sea but it was too rough and he drowned.

Next month, on 13th June, the squadron became involved with the FW190s of III./JG 2 while escorting Venturas to St.Brieuc. Flying Officer Jan Stastny got one of the FW190s in his gun sight however another

Spitfire VB EP660/DU-O. During Summer 1942, it was Pilot Officer V. Slouf's mount. (Jiri Rajlich)

Two sections of Spitfire VBs, with cropped wings, passing over Skeabrae airfield in 1943. (Jiri Rajlich)

enemy aircraft then scored hits on his Spitfire. Jan Stastny managed to return to Church Stanton but his aircraft had received Category B damage. The squadron's last action before being pulled out of the line was *Ramrod* 100 which covered the withdrawal of B-17s which had bombed airfields at Villacoublay and Bernay St. Martin on 23ʳᵈ June 1943.

Next day the Squadron's personnel were transported, on board the Handley Page Harrows of No.271 squadron, to their new base Skaebrae on the Orkney Islands, where they changed places with No.234 squadron as the fighter defence of the the Royal Navy's Home Fleet base at Scapa Flow.

Between 7ᵗʰ July and 10ᵗʰ July, B Flight was detached to the airfield at Sumburgh and on 19ᵗʰ August the Commanding Officer of No.14 Group Air Vice Marshall Raymond Collishaw, posted eight Spitfires of A Flight to the airfield at Peterhead near Aberdeen. From time to time reconnaissance Ju88s would appear however they usually managed to escape interception but on 27ᵗʰ August the squadron carried out a successful attack on one of these aircraft. At 1747 hours Flight Lieutenant Karel Kasal and Flying Officer Karel Posta took off for a standing patrol over the sea some 30 miles east of Peterhead. After an hour they spotted a Ju88D-5 at a height of about 30 ft above the sea and Kasal, followed by Posta, attacked and the Junkers crashed into the sea 80 miles north-east of the

base. This was the only confirmed victory gained by No.312 Squadron in 1943. On 1ˢᵗ July Flight Lieutenant Vaclav Slouf succeeded Viktor Kaslik as the leader of B Flight.

No.453 (RAAF) Squadron arrived to replace No.312 Squadron on 21ˢᵗ September which then moved to its new base at Ibsley where all the Czechoslovak fighter squadrons were again brought together as a wing.

Their first task, *Ramrod* 83, on 22ⁿᵈ September, was to escort twelve Mitchells to and from the airfield at Guipavas. Next day No.312 Squadron carried out two operations, the first in conjunction with No.313 Squadron, and then *Ramrod* 85, a patrol over Lannion, Morlaix and the Batz Island. Subsequently the whole Wing escorted eighteen Mitchells to bomb Poulmic-Lanveoc airfield. *Ramrods* 87 and 88 were carried out on 24ᵗʰ September and on two occasions on the 26ᵗʰ they escorted B-26 Marauders of 8ᵗʰ Air Force to attack Luftwaffe airfields. During these raids the Wing claimed several victories but none fell to No.312 Squadron.

The Squadron carried out nine escort operations in October. During *Ramrod* 95 on 25ᵗʰ October they lost their second pilot of the year. Before noon the squadron moved from Ibsley to Portreath and at 1326 hours took off to escort twenty-four Mitchells on a raid on Poulmic-Lanveoc airfield near Brest. Heavy flak shot down two Mitchells and Flying Officer Jan

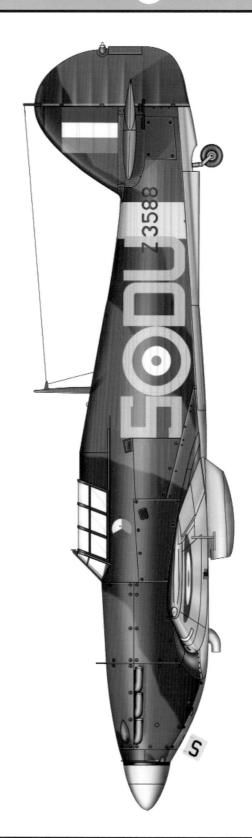

Hawker Hurricane Mk.IIB Z3588, No.312 (Czechoslovak) Squadron, Flying Officer T. Vybiral, Kenley, June 1941.

Stastny. He baled out and descended into the sea 50 miles south of Lizzard Point but the Supermarine Walruses of the ASR squadron failed to find him. Squadron Leader Tomas Vybiral was replaced as commanding officer on 1st November by Squadron Leader Frantisek Vancl and the Squadron continued escorting bombers and attacking targets on the continent, however flying bomb launch sites were now the priority targets. These operations were named *Noballs*.

WITH THE 2ND TAF

The 2nd Tactical Air Force was established in November and the Czechoslovak Wing was incorporated into this formation on 7th January, 1944. This change foreshadowed the re-equipment of the squadron with the latest versions of the Spitfire, however No.312 Squadron had to continue with Spitfire VBs for the immediate future.

During November the Squadron escorted nine bomber raids to targets in France without major incident except on 26th November, during *Ramrod* 110, whilst they escorting twenty-four Mitchells, the Czechs encountered enemy aircraft in the vicinity of Cherbourg. A lone FW190 escaped when it was attacked by Flight Lieutenant Kasal and Warrant Officer Oldrich Vychodil. December began with the Czechoslovak squadrons flying as top cover for 52 B-26s on a raid on the airfield at Cambrai-Epinoy on the 1st. The next flights over the continent were carried out late in December. These were raids on V-1 launch sites; Dieppe, on the 21st, Abbeville on the 23rd and 24th and Cherbourg on the 30th. On the 31st the squadron escorted 72 B-26s to a *Noball* site near Amiens.

The Squadron's first Spitfire LF.IXcs were delivered on 10th January 1944 and as operations had to continue during the changeover it was not completed until the middle of February. On 1st February Wing Commander Tomas Vybiral, formerly commander of No.312 squadron, became the Officer Commanding No.134 Airfield and on 20th February the squadron was transferred to Mendlesham in Suffolk. The first operation carried out with its new Spitfires was *Ramrod* 621 on 4th March when, together with No.310 Squadron, it escorted 18 Havocs to *Noball* sites near Maisoncelle.

Between 5th and 14th March the Wing, together with No.132 (Norwegian) Airfield, took part in the Exercise *Lambourne I* in which the pilots were trained in attacking armoured vehicles and other ground targets. Back on operations on 15th March they escorted 72 B-26s over Belgium. On 23rd March the Czechoslovak squadrons had a busy day. The first operation of the day, *Ramrod* 677, saw them escorting two dozen Mitchells to the marshalling yard at Creil in France, then at 1625 hours 36 Spitfires, led by Wing Commander Tomas Vybiral, escorted 72 B-26s of 9th Air Force on a raid on the marshalling yard at Haine St. Pierre near La Louvier. On the return journey the Squadron was attacked by seven FW190s of I./JG 26 and Flying Officer Ladislav Svetlik got the tail of a FW190 pursuing another Spitfire. The German was aware of the danger but was too late in responding and Svetlik fired twice, obliging the

Spitfire VB EN793/DU-C taking off from Ibsley for another mission during the winter of 1943 - 1944. At that time the Squadron flew only a handful of operational sorties. (Jiri Rajlich).

German pilot to bale out. During this operation the Spitfire flown by Pilot Officer Frantisek Mlejnecky was hit by *flak* and had to make a belly landing at Manston. Three days later the squadron escorted 108 B-26s and on 27th and 28th, together with No.313 Squadron, they escorted Marauders again.

The Squadron moved to the airfield at Appledram and the first operation carried out from this airfield was *Ramrod* 710 on 8th April. During the following days the Squadron's pilots practised dive bombing with 500 lb bombs.

On 15th April the squadron strafed the airfield at Dreux and on the 18th escorted 36 B-26s to bomb the depot at Charleroi and then, on 19th April, the pilots attacked *Noball* sites near Neufchâtel from which they returned without loss. In the afternoon they flew as close escort for 72 B-26s. As the Wing, led Wing Commander T. Vybiral, approached the target they were attacked by twenty Bf109s, then eight FW190s of I./JG 26 joined the attack. The Squadron lost Flight Lieutenant Bohuslav Budil, who was probably hit by *Major* Karl Borris. Bohuslav Budil baled out and landed directly in front of a concrete fortification off Diksmuide and was captured.

Next day the Squadron escorted bombers to V-1 launch sites near Pas-de-Calais and similar targets near Abbeville. On 21st April General Dwight D. Eisenhower, and his staff, visited the Squadron now based at No.134 Airfield so the Squadron carried out only one operation that day - an attack on *Noball*

sites near Abbeville. Attacks against V-1 launch sites were carried out between 25th April and 1st May after which they took part in Exercise *Lambourne II* and undertook training in co-operating with ground troops and attacks on transports. When the Squadron returned to operational duty it continued its previous dive bombing attacks and escorting bombers to targets in France.

In May the Squadron took part in eleven attacks on *Noball* sites, strafed another eight targets and escorted medium bombers on six occasions. Two pilots were lost on 15th May when, after the squadron had returned from *Ramrod* 887, two Spitfires collided on the airfield. Flying Officer Ladislav Svetlik, who had just landed, crashed into a taxiing Spitfire, whose pilot Warrant Officer Antonin Prvonic was mortally injured and died after being taken to the first-aid station. Squadron Leader Jaroslav Hlado became the Squadron's new Commanding Officer on this day.

On 21st May, during *Ramrod* 905, the Czechoslovak Wing strafed various targets in Normandy. Blue Section, led by Flying Officer Vladimir Kopecek, attacked targets between St. Malo and Le Havre and at 1100 hours the Spitfire of Flight Sergeant Robert Ossendorf was hit. He made an emergency landing 11 kilometres east of Aire, and managed to escape and, although wounded, fought with the Maquis for a month before returning to the UK. The French General Koenig subsequently awarded him the *Croix de Guerre* "For bravery in combat". Flying

MK483/VY, a Spitfire LF.IXC was the personal mount of Wing Commander Tomas Vybiral when he was leading No.134 (Czechoslovak) Wing during the spring of 1944. (Jiri Rajlich)

A somewhat weathered Spitfire VB W3249 "Baltic Exchange III" arrived at No.312 Squadron on 10.12.41. It remained with the unit until September 1942. (Andrew Thomas)

THE SUPERMARINE SPITFIRE

The Supermarine Spitfire was the main RAF fighter during World War II, and the only British fighter to remain in production throughout. It made its maiden flight on 5th March 1936 powered by a Rolls-Royce 990 hp Merlin C engine. Suitably impressed, the Air Ministry placed an order in July and mass production of the Spitfire Mk.I, powered with a Rolls-Royce Merlin II 1,030 hp engine, commenced.

It entered service in August 1938 and ten squadrons were operational at the outbreak of war. During the Battle of France a few Spitfires flew reconnaissance flights, although its first serious test took place during the evacuation of Dunkirk.

During the Battle of Britain it proved superior to the Hurricane and was to remain the RAF's principal fighter until the end of the war. The improved **Spitfire Mk.II**, powered by a 1,175 hp Merlin XII, appeared in August 1940 and was, in turn, replaced by the **Spitfire Mk.V** during the spring of 1941. This version, powered by a 1,470 hp Merlin 45, was better armed and was the first of the two dominant variants of the Spitfire. It did however have serious problems contending with the FW190 when it subsequently appeared.

The **Spitfire Mk.IX**, the second major variant (1,650 hp Merlin 63) arrived in July 1942, to arrest the situation for the RAF, but it was not until well into 1943 that it appeared in sufficient enough numbers to gain a measure of superiority.

A second generation of Spitfires appeared during 1944, when the Rolls-Royce Griffon engine, capable of delivering upwards of 2,000 hp, was developed. However these only partially replaced the Merlin-powered marks already in service.

From March 1942 Spitfires were sent overseas in increasing numbers and by the end of the war were present in all RAF theatres of operation. Both generations of Spitfire were widely used in the post-war RAF until jet aircraft fully replaced them during the early fifties.

2ND TACTICAL AIR FORCE

Following the Desert Air Force's success in North Africa, in its support of the British 8th Army, the RAF decided to create a similar structure to support ground forces that were gathering in the British Isles to carry out the planned Invasion of Europe. This resulted in the creation of the 2nd Tactical Air Force on 1st June 1943 with the RAF having to draw upon elements of Fighter, Bomber and Army Co-Operation Commands, to form the new command. Army Co-operation Command was considered obsolete and effectively dissolved.

Plans for the invasion began to gain momentum in the spring of 1943 after the surrender of the Axis forces in North Africa had freed up Allied troops. Until then the RAF in Britain had been organised in such a way that only Army Co-operation Squadrons were able to give direct support to the Army. Initially the 2nd Tactical Air Force was responsible to Fighter Command, but it became fully autonomous on 15th November and fell under the structure of the newly formed Allied Expeditionary Air Force. The task allocated to 2nd TAF was simple- it was to provide support to the 21st Army Group, which incorporated all the Commonwealth ground units that were to take part in the invasion. This Army Group was itself divided into two Armies - the 2nd British and the 1st Canadian.

By D-Day, the 2nd Tactical Air Force consisted of :

<u>No.2 Group</u> : Formerly part of Bomber Command its ten light and medium bomber squadrons, which specialised in daylight bombing, were transferred to 2nd TAF control on 1st June 1943. At the time its squadrons were equipped with Bostons, Mitchells and Venturas, although those operating Venturas were fully re-equipped with Mosquito FB.VIs by September. By the time the invasion began No.2 Group had been enlarged to 12 squadrons arranged under four Wings.

<u>No.83 Group</u> : Created on 1st April 1943 as part of Fighter Command, it passed into 2nd TAF control on 1st June 1943. Its role was to provide support to the 2nd British Army and by D-Day it consisted of 29 combat squadrons, under ten Wings, and four Air Observation Post (AOP) Squadrons, under an 11th Wing.

<u>No.84 Group</u> : Created on the 15th July 1943 to give aerial support to the 1st Canadian Army. By D-Day it consisted of 29 combat squadrons under 10 Wings, and three AOP Squadrons under an 11th Wing.

<u>No.85 Group</u> : Created on the 2nd December 1943, to provide aerial protection, particularly at night, to that region in which the Invasion force was being prepared. By D-Day this Group consisted of 12 combat squadrons (an even mix of night and day fighters) arranged under five Wings. It also included an Air Spotting Pool containing a further seven squadrons - four from the Fleet Air Arm, one from the US Navy and two Tactical Reconnaissance - and a Flight. By October 1944 the Battle line had moved well away from UK bases and this Group was relegated a Maintenance and Training Group.

<u>No.87 Group</u> : Created on 17th February 1945 to take over control of units in the Paris and Southern French zones.

<u>Headquarters</u> : Headquarters 2nd TAF also had under its umbrella a three-squadron Reconnaissance Wing and a Meteorological Flight.

In preparation for D-Day No 312 Squadron was re-equipped with Spitfire IXs. MJ931/DU-L was usually flown by Flying Officer L. Svetlik. (Jiri Rajlich)

Officer Miroslav Liskutin's aircraft was badly damaged in combat on 21st May but he managed to fly it back to Appledram. During an attack on a column of lorries he had brushed one wing of his Spitfire against a tree. The Squadron's last action before D-Day was a *Ramrod* on 2nd June when two trains were attacked near Vire.

THE LIBERATION OF EUROPE

No.134 (Czechoslovak) Wing was at operational readiness at 0430 hours on 6th June and at 0720 hours 36 Spitfires took off to patrol the Normandy beaches. In sections of four aircraft the Squadron flew between Bernieres and Cabourg. Beneath them on *Juno* Beach the Canadians of 3rd Infantry Division and 2nd Armoured Brigade fought the 716 *Infanterie Division* and 21*Panzer Division*. On the first day of the invasion the Squadron performed four patrols over the Normandy beaches at 0720 - 0915 hours, 1225 - 1425 hours, 1700 - 1820 hours and 2100 - 2235 hours however they did not see any enemy aircraft and all their aircraft returned.

Next day the Squadron flew four sorties. During the second the Czechoslovak pilots came into contact with 16 FW190 fighter bombers north of Caen. No.312 Squadron attacked the closest formation of eight FW190s however they escaped. Sergeant Jindrich Konvicka left the formation and pursued the enemy. He managed to fire five short bursts into one of the Focke-Wulfs from a range of 350 yards before it disappeared into the clouds. This aircraft was credited as damaged and Flying Officer Vladimir Kopecek, was also credited with one damaged.

Another four patrols were carried out on 8th June. The second patrol, comprising 36 Spitfires, led by Wing

Commander Jan Cermak who formerly commanded No.312 Squadron, took off at 1220 hours. The squadron was patrolling east of Caen when at 1335 hours the controller warned them of enemy aircraft in the vicinity. The pilots spotted a dozen FW190s, which had just bombed *Sword* Beach. No.312 Squadron attacked immediately and Wing Commander Cermak, chased six of the enemy into the clouds. From a range of 350 yards his bullets hit one FW190 and its pilot baled out.

He then scored hits on another Focke-Wulf but it managed to escape into the clouds. His Number 2, Sergeant Vit Angetter fired three short bursts into a FW190 which crashed into the sea five miles north of Courseulles-sur-Mer. An additional four FW190s were also claimed as damaged. Flying Officer Frantisek Kopecek claimed two while Pilot Officer Frantisek Mlejnecky and Warrant Officer Antonin Skach each claimed one. All the Squadron's aircraft returned at 1420 hours and next day all flights were cancelled by bad weather.

On 10th June the Squadron carried out four operations over the beachhead and during an afternoon´flight Flight Sergeant Jindrich Konvicka attacked a lone Bf109G and after a short chase in the clouds the two aircraft almost collided when the left wing of Konvicka´s Spitfire hit the tail fin of a Messerschmitt. Konvicka's aircraft survived this contact but was hit by *flak* near Caen and he landed in the Channel 5 miles north of the town where he was picked up by an ASR boat. Next day three patrols were carried out but due to bad weather and fog two aircraft, and one pilot, were lost during the last patrol of the day.

Nine Spitfires landed at Appledram around 1835 hours all with virtually empty fuel tanks. The pilots of Red Section led by Flight Lieutenant Vojtech Smolik

SERIALS OF SPITFIRE IX IN USE ON 6TH JUNE 1944.

MH : 474, 499
MJ : 553, 572, 751, 792, 799, 840, 881, 940
MK : 180, 244, 449, 483, 580, 775, 805, 895, 912
NH : 546

Total : 20

failed to find their own airfield. Vojtech Smolik made a belly landing north of Worthing when he ran out of petrol and his Number 2, Sergeant Vilem Nosek, crashed into a hill near Washington north-east of the base. Two other pilots spotted the Airspeed factory airfield through a hole in the clouds and Flight Lieutenant Frantisek Truhlar attempted to land however his engine cut out during the final approach and his undercarriage brushed against the fence. The Spitfire crashed and burst into flames and S.W. Thomas, of the Portsmouth Fire Brigade, and P. Mitchell, the workshop manager, risked their lives to pull him out of the cockpit. Flight Sergeant Vaclav Soukup, Truhlar´s wing man landed successfully.

During the following days the Squadron flew combat patrols over the beaches or convoys of ships sailing towards Normandy. For a change No.312 Squadron escorted Lancasters and Halifaxes heavy bombers on a raid against the *Noball* sites near Boulogne and

Siracourt on 21st and 22nd June. The Squadron then relocated to Tangmere on 22nd June and three days later it made an attack on Chartres airfield and in conjunction with the other squadrons of No.134 Wing they escorted one hundred RAF bombers to V-1 launch sites near Abbeville. At 0750 hours on 28th June 1944 Wing Commander Tomas Vybiral led No.134 Wing to France and their new base at B-10, near Plumetôt village, and the Squadron carried out its first operations from French soil. Taking off on *Ramrod* 1050 at 1915 hours on 30th June the Czechoslovak Wing escorted 151 Lancasters and 105 Halifaxs to attack units German units some 25 kilometres west of Caen.

Between 1st and 10th July the Squadron escorted heavy bombers of Bomber Command to targets in France on no less than nine occasions then on 3rd July the squadron was transferred to Air Defence Great Britain and took up residence at Lympne where it exchanged its

Spitfire LF IXC MJ840/DU-L with invasion bands. This aircraft was lost on 11.06.44 and its pilot, Sergeant Vilem Nosek, was killed. (Jiri Rajlich)

RECRUITMENT PROBLEMS

Even though the Czechoslovaks, like the Poles, had arrived in the United Kingdom during the summer of 1940, in sufficient numbers to form three Squadrons (two fighters and one bomber), the Czechoslovakian Government in exile were soon to be faced with a recruiting problem. Although the number of Air Force personnel remained constant from 1940 to 1944 at around 1,600 men and women there was a critical lack of ground crew. In July 1940 about 575 flying personnel arrived in the United Kingdom but only 250 mechanics. The Czechoslovaks had been numerous enough to fight alongside the French, and at one point they had been able to raise an Infantry division, so it would seem that many of these men chose voluntary demobilisation after the Armistice. The airmen who came to the United Kingdom in the summer of 1940 were either flying officers or senior NCOs instead of the lower ranks. The shortage of the latter was to plague the CzAF throughout the war. As early as 1941, the problem was raised by both the RAF and the CIG as it was obvious that new personnel would be needed to replace losses, or just to allow a turn over of personnel in the operational units. As it was, the Czechoslovakian units were dramatically lacking in ground crew from their own nation and this, at a later date, was to jeopardise the existence of No.313 Squadron despite there being enough Czechoslovakian pilots available to be posted in. In February 1941 85% of the ground crew in No.310 Squadron were Czechoslovaks, but only 50% in the case of No.312 Squadron. In these conditions a political agreement was signed to allow the creation of No.313 Squadron with the majority of its ground crew coming from British sources and this led to the establishment of a full Czechoslovak fighter wing. The RAF insisted that Czechoslovak Army personnel enlist in the RAF as ground crew for No.313 Squadron, however the Czechoslovak Government in exile was against this idea as their Army was also facing problems in obtaining men to maintain its numbers. The Army was too small to be involved in any large scale actions and until 1943 was limited to just Middle East operations.

As replacement personnel could not be obtained from Czechoslovakia, other sources were tried. Three were investigated, two countries in North America, Britain and the land forces in the Middle East. The Czechoslovakian Government had real hopes of obtaining volunteers from Canada, but the Canadians did not encourage any Czechoslovaks, nor Poles for that matter, to enlist in the RAF. Only a handful of men were recruited in Canada and the United States of America mainly because of lack of publicity and political support from Canada or the United Kingdom. It also proved difficult to motivate people to fight for a country they had chosen to leave many years previously. For those reasons the Czechoslovak units had to be used carefully, to avoid seeing the units disbanded due to a lack of personnel. However their fighting spirit remained intact throughout the war and if their military value was less than could have been obtained the publicity given to the Czechoslovakian units played a major role in the political field.

aircraft for the Spitfire HF.IXs of No.74 Squadron. The Czechoslovak Wing now found itself trying to intercept V-1s but the Squadron's aircraft were not fast enough to catch them and no successes were claimed. Eight days later the squadron moved to Coltishall and Flight Lieutenant O. Smik became B Flight's leader. The squadron's targets were now mostly situated in the Netherlands and on 16th July they began with attacks on the harbour at Ijmunden and then Hilversum. A week later the squadron carried out a reconnaissance flight over Rotterdam Harbour and, on 26th July, it escorted twenty-four Bristol Beaufighters over Den Helden and then performed reconnaissance flights over the harbours at Ijmunden and Rotterdam. During August the Squadron had a change of targets and concentrated on attacking trains and the railway tracks. *Ranger* 27 was carried out on 11th August when the Squadron operated between

Eindhoven and Rotterdam. Yellow section - Flying Officer Kopecek, Sergeant Gibian, Flight Sergeant Ocelka and Sergeant Pristupa - attacked the railway station at Arendonk and destroyed a locomotive however when Gustav Pristupa pulled out of his dive he struck an electrical cable and then some trees. Pristupa was able to make a crash landing in a field but his Spitfire turned over and burst into flames. He managed to get out of the cockpit but the Canadian of Czech origin was captured. It was believed that his external fuel tank had not been released.

On 14th August they took off from Manston on *Rodeo* 9 and during this operation No.312 Squadron flew over German territory for the first time when it patrolled over the town of Wessel. Near Homberg the pilots spotted a group of seven FW190s but the Germans avoided combat. The Squadron lost another pilot on 25th August. At 1755 hours a section of four Spitfires,

Spitfire HF.IXC MK670 DU-Y, flown by Sergent V. Angetter participated in a raid on Raalte on 25.08.44. (Jiri Raljich)

led by Flight Lieutenant Smik, took off to carry out a *Ranger* operation. The target was the airfield at Steenwijk but when they flew over the target they saw no activity and continued towards Zwolle. Here they spotted three trains in the railway station at Raalte and Smik, Warrant Officer Vaclav Ruprecht, Flight Sergeant Jindrich Konvicka and Sergeant Vit Angetter attacked one of these and the target burst into flames which immediately spread to the other two trains. During the return flight the engine of Warrant Officer Ruprecht's Spitfire failed when he switched over from the external fuel tank to the main tank and the aircraft crashed into the Channel 60 miles east of Great Yarmouth at 1945 hours.

The Squadron moved to North Weald on 27th August and on the same day, along with No.310 Squadron, they escorted 229 bombers of the RAF to the refinery in Meerbeck. In August No.312 Squadron carried out a total of six escorts and September started with an attack on targets in the vicinity of Calais, Ghent and Lille then continued by escorting Mitchells attacking V-2 sites near St. Omer and finally the marshalling yard at Givet. The Squadron sustained heavy losses during *Ramrod* 1258 on 3rd September when they escorted 100 Halifaxes to bomb Soesterberg airfield which was a German night fighter base. Blue Section, led by Flight Lieutenant Otto Smik, asked for permission to attack camouflaged Ju88s on the airfield at Gilze-Rijen then

dived from 10,000 feet followed by Sergeant Vratislav Liska, Flying Officer Jaroslav Sodek and Sergeant Alois Stanc. The airfield's anti-aircraft defences opened up on the Spitfires and Smik set fire to one Ju88 but then reported that he had been hit and that he would have to bale out. However he was able to make an emergency landing near Priesenbeek, north of Breda, and escaped being captured. Dutch civilians hid him and on 26th October Smik crossed the front line and three days later he returned to England.

MARKET-GARDEN

Operation *Market-Garden* started on 17th September 1944. At 1215 hours on the 17th Nos.310 and 312 Squadrons, under the command of Wing Comamnder Tomas Vybiral, escorted 1,545 transport aircraft and 478 gliders to the drop zone at Nijmegen and then strafed Standaarbirish gun posts before returning to North Weald at 1505.

Next day No.312 Squadron, along with Nos.310 and 234 Squadrons, took off at 1305 hours and the Wing, again led by the WingCo escorted transport aircraft and gliders to the bridge at Moersdijk near Nijmegen. During the return flight anti-aircraft batteries at Willensdorp fired at them and hit the oil cooler on CO's aircraft, however he managed to return to base. Flight Sergeant Antonin Ocelka was less lucky as his Spitfire was also hit in the engine and he had to make an emergency landing near Strijen. The aircraft was wrecked and he was seriously injured however he was helped by local people, who were unfortunately unable to attend to his wounded eye. A local doctor advised him that he should go to the local hospital in Breda and subsequently he was moved to the hospital in Münster and then to the PoW camp in Bankau. For the next two days the Squadron escorted transports and gliders to Eindhoven. With the failure of Operation *Market Garden* No.312 Squadron returned to bomber escort duties.

The squadron moved to Bradwell Bay on 3rd October 1944 and there, together with Nos.64 and 126 Squadrons, they formed a wing under the command of Wing Commander H. Bird-Wilson. As part of this Wing No.312 Squadron escorted bombers on day raids which were now mostly targets in Germany. On 18th October, while escorting 128 Lancasters to Bonn, some pilots sighted a group of Me262s which they tried to attack but the jets refused to be drawn into a fight and withdrew.

Wing Commander Jaroslav Hlado took over command of the Czechoslovak Wing on 15th November and Squadron Leader Vaclav Slouf, the leader of A

Flight, assumed command of the Squadron while Flight Lieutenant Karel Posta replaced him as A Flight's leader. In November No.64 Squadron had become the first squadron of the Bradwell Wing to receive North American Mustang IIIs and were followed some time later by No.126 Squadron. No.312 Squadron was expecting to receive this type of aircraft however on 29th December Nos.64 and 126 Squadrons were posted to Bentwaters and Nos.310 and 313 Squadrons arrived to replace them.

While the Squadron was returning from a raid on Duisburg on 14th October Flight Sergeant Jindrich Bilek crash-landed at B-80 (Volkel) when he ran out of fuel. The squadron then lost the Spitfire flown Flight Lieutenant Jiri Mikulecky on 21st October who was hit by enemy ground fire and crashed south-east of Terneuzen. Twelve *Ramrods* were carried out in November when the Squadron escorted bombers to targets on German territory. On 8th December at 1010 hours a dozen Spitfires of No.312 Squadron took off on *Ramrod* 1401, and in thick fog, Spitfire of Flight Sergeant Josef Skrinar collided with Sergeant Anton Vanko's machine, and both Spitfires burst into flames. Skrinar managed to escape from his burning aircraft but Vanko, who had become famous as the result of his escape from Slovakia to Turkey, in an Avia B-71,

Spitfire F.IXC MH367 DU-Z at Manston during the winter of 1944-45. (Jiri Rajlich)

On 01.02.45, Spitfire IX BS458/DU-F ran out of fuel while returning from escorting Lancasters. Its pilot, 2nd Lieutenant A Gaydos, made an emergency landing during which he sustained serious injuries. (Jiri Rajlich)

on 18th April 1943, died in his aircraft.

Of the 10 Spitfires which took off seven made an early return to the airfield and an eighth had to make an emergency landing near Bruxelles. Bomber Command's targets were now deep in Germany so the Czechoslovak squadrons were transferred to allied airfields B-65, B-67 and B-90 in Belgium, and B-86 in the Netherlands, to cut down unnecessary flying time. In spite of this, lack of fuel was the cause of the loss of Flight Lieutenant Zdenek Donda on 31st December. While he was escorting 158 Lancasters to the marshalling yard in Vohwinkel, near Solingen, he ran out of fuel and tried to land on B-67 (Ursel) however he crashed near Kortenboeken. He was pulled out of the cockpit and rushed to the hospital at Sevel-Seget where he died of his injuries.

The first sortie in 1945 was *Ramrod* 1427 on 5th January. During the outward flight American North American P-51s and Republic P-47s attacked the Squadron. Fortunately this misunderstanding was soon cleared up and no Spitfires were hit. However during the return flight on 1st February 1945, 2nd Lieutenant Albert Gaydos, an American of Slovakian origin ran out of fuel. He managed to make a belly landing on his own airfield, however the aircraft was heavily damaged and he sustained serious injuries.

The Czechoslovak Wing carried out another two escorts in January and twelve in February without any operational losses, however on the afternoon of 9th February Pilot Officer Alois Zalesky, dived to the earth west of Manston for unknown reasons and was killed. Half an hour later Sergeant Ondrej Samberger lost consciousness at 33,000 ft, probably due of the

failure of his oxygen supply, and crashed into the sea 80 miles north-east of Bradwell Bay. These were to be the last of the squadron's wartime fatal casualties.

On 27th February 1945 the Wing transferred to Manston and in March the squadron carried out 18 operations. On 11th March three pilots, Squadron Leader Vaclav Slouf, Warrant Officer Bedrich Holzner and Flight Sergeant Josef Kukucka, escorted a Dakota of No.24 Squadron which was carrying President Eduard Benes of the Czechoslovak Republic. This aircraft was taking the President, together with the members of the Government in Exile, to the Soviet Union. They escorted him on the first part of his journey from Northolt to St. Valery-en-Caux.

In April pilots of the squadron flew seven sorties and the squadron's last wartime sortie, *Ramrod* 1546, was carried out on 19th April. On 6th May 1945 pilots of the squadron learned about the uprising in Prague and immediately began to organise aid for the partisans who were attacking German in their homeland. On 7th May the pilots of No.312 Squadron were sitting in the cockpits of their Spitfires waiting for the order to take off at 1745 hours however the planned flight to Pilsen was cancelled by General Dwight Eisenhower.

After five year of flights the Squadron finally landed in its liberated country on 13th August 1945. On 22nd September the squadron moved to Ceské Budejovice where it became the basis of the 2.*letecka divize* (2nd Air Division), opening a new era for the Czechoslovak Air Force. No.312 (Czechoslovak) Squadron was officially disbanded by the RAF on 15th February 1946.

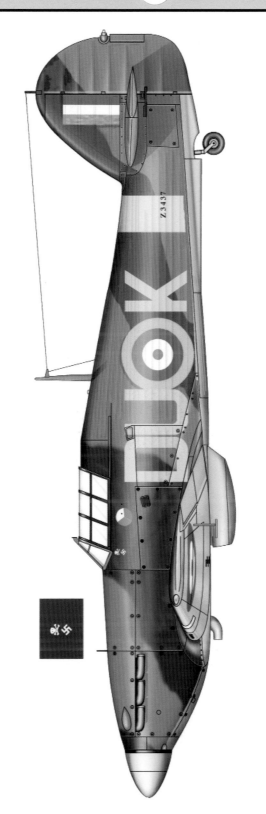

Hawker Hurricane Mk.IIB Z3437, No.312 (Czechoslovak) Squadron, Flight Sergeant O. Kucera, Ayr, August 1941.

Spitfire LF.IXC MJ799/DU-I under maintenance at Appledram in 1944. (Jiri Rajlich)

No.312 (Czechoslovak) Squadron

Authorized H.M. King George VI : July 1942

CODE : DU

Formed	Disbanded
29.08.40	15.02.46

DESCRIPTION
A stork *volant*

MOTTO
NON MULTI SED MULTA

NOT MANY BUT MUCH

SIGNIFICANCE OF DESIGN

The stork in the badge relates to the French *"Escadrille des Cigognes"* with whom the original pilots of No.312 Squadron had flown prior to coming to the United Kingdom.

Squadron Leader Frank H. Tyson was the first and only British Commanding Officer of No.312 Squadron and this was his last operational command during the war.

SQUADRON COMMANDERS

S/L F.H. TYSON*	29.08.40 - 01.04.41
S/L E. CIZEK	01.04.41 - 27.05.41
S/L J. KLAN	27.05.41 - 08.06.41
S/L A. VASATKO	08.06.41 - 01.05.42
S/L J. CERMAK	01.05.42 - 01.01.43
S/L T. VYBIRAL	01.01.43 - 01.11.43
S/L F. VANCL	01.11.43 - 15.05.44
S/L J. HLADO	15.05.44 - 15.11.44
S/L V. SLOUF	15.11.44 - 19.04.45
S/L H. HRBACEK	19.04.45 - 13.08.45

*British.

OPERATIONAL DATA

NUMBER OF SORTIES

	Hurr. I	Hurr. II	Spit. II	Spit. V	Spit. VII	Spit. IX	Total
First sortie	04.10.40	04.06.41	-	31.12.41	08.09.43	04.02.44	
Last sortie	30.05.41	12.12.41	-	29.01.44	08.09.43	22.04.45	
Total by type	1,189	1,336	-	5,797	5	2,887	11,013
Aircraft lost	9	4	1	13	-	20	47
Claims (Conf. & Prob.)	2	8	-	8.5	-	4	22.5

NUMBER OF PILOTS LOST

	Hurr. I	Hurr. II	Spit. II	Spit. V	Spit. VII	Spit. IX	Total
Killed	4	-	1	5	-	7	17
PoW	-	1	-	2	-	2	5
Evaded	-	1	-	-	-	2	3

BREAKDOWN OF PILOTS KILLED BY CITIZENSHIP

British :	1
Czechoslovaks :	16

DETAILS OF THE FIRST AND LAST MISSION (SERIAL, NAME, TIME OF DEPARTURE AND RETURN)

04.10.40

Scramble

P2575/P	S/L F.H. Tyson	1050	1135
L1807	F/L D.E. Gillam	1050	1145
L1926/J	P/O A. Vasatko	1050	1145
L1822	P/O V. Vesely	1050	1145
L1740/O	Sgt F. Chabera	1050	1135
L1841/H	S/L J. Ambrus	1050	1135

22.04.45

Weather recce

BS384/E	W/O J. Bilek	0620	0825
MH332	F/Sgt J. Zarecky	0620	0825

MAJOR AWARDS*

DSO	DFC	DFM
NONE	8	1

DFC : 8
BAR : NONE

*For security reasons most of the awards received by citizens of occupied Europe were not published in the London Gazette. This was to avoid any kind of vengeance attacks being made on next-of-kin who remained in their homeland.

HIGHER COMMANDS

FIGHTER COMMAND
Duxford Sector, No.12 Group
29.08.40/26.09.40

Speke Sector, No.9 Group
26.09.40/03.03.41

Valley Sector, No.9 Group
03.03.41/25.04.41

Jurby Sector, No.9 Group
25.04.41/29.05.41

Kenley Sector, No.11 Group
29.05.41/20.07.41

Debden Sector, No.11 Group
20.07.41/19.08.41

Ayr Sector, No.13 Group
19.08.41/01.01.42

Fairwood Common Sector, No.10 Group
01.01.42/20.04.42

Middle Wallop Sector, No.10 Group
20.04.42/24.04.42

Fairwood Common Sector, No.10 Group
24.04.42/02.05.42

Exeter Sector, No.10 Group
02.05.42/19.05.42

Middle Wallop Sector, No.10 Group
19.05.42/31.05.42

Exeter Sector, No.10 Group
31.05.42/01.07.42

Kenley Sector, No.11 Group
01.07.42/08.07.42

Exeter Sector, No.10 Group
08.07.42/16.08.42

Kenley Sector, No.11 Group
16.08.42/20.08.42

Exeter Sector, No.10 Group
20.08.42/20.02.43

Middle Wallop Sector, No.10 Group
20.02.43/14.03.43

Exeter Sector, No.10 Group
14.03.43/24.06.43

Kirkwall Sector, No.14 Group
24.06.43/21.09.43

Middle Wallop Sector, No.10 Group
21.09.43/15.11.43

ADGB
Middle Wallop Sector, No.10 Group
15.11.43/02.12.43

Valley Sector, No.9 Group
02.12.43/18.12.43

Middle Wallop Sector, No.10 Group
18.12.43/19.02.44

2ND TACTICAL AIR FORCE
No.134 (Czechoslovak) Airfield, No.84 Group
19.02.44/12.05.44

No.134 (Czechoslovak) Wing, No.84 Group
12.05.44/29.06.44

ADGB/FIGHTER COMMAND
No.134 (Czechoslovak) Wing, No.11 Group
29.06.44/11.07.44

Coltishall Sector, No.12 Group
11.07.44/27.08.44

North Weald Sector, No.11 Group
27.08.44/29.12.44

Czech Wing, No.11 Group
29.12.44/24.08.45

Known individual letters

A : AR550, BL260, BS508, EN841, MJ907, ML148, TE566
B : P8570, W9137*, AB372, BL231, EP240, EP518, EP547, MJ637, SL627
C : AD572, BL254, EN793, EP539, MA467, MK682, NH546, TE522
D : AD553, BS125, EP435, LZ951, MK608, MK805, TE575
E : Z3467*, AD553, AR501, BS384, EE721, EP564, MJ881, MK694
F : V6930*, BS458, ML195, TE524
G : BS433, MH322, SL654
H : L1841*, BM145, ML240
I : AB939, BL626, EP570, ML799, ML174
J : Z3314*, L1926*, V6943*, AA970, AR319, BL231, BL470, EP558, MH354, MJ726, MJ840, MK940
K : V7063*, W3249, Z3437*, MH830, MJ553, SL633
L : V6678*, Z3221*, Z3242*, BL381, EP785, MJ840, ML230, ML931, SL625
M : P3268*, EN866
N : V6848*, P3612*, W3798, BL512, EP518, MH352, ML296, NH250
O : L1740*, P3888*, AB172, AR519, EP125, EP660, MA834, ML195, NH148

Spitfire VB EP660/DU-O being serviced by groundcrew during Summer 1942.
(C.J. Ehrengardt)

P : P2575*, P3965*, P7567, W3230*, Z2836*, BL343, BS129, EP352, MJ893, MJ895, MK895, ML261, SL631
Q : P3983*, AB505, MH314, SL649
R : V6921*, P8081, X4106, Z3221*, BL289, EP432, MH832, MJ499, MK248, MK449, ML245, NH450, SL626
S : P3209*, V6930*, P7698, W3837, Z3588*, BM229, BM322, EP564, MH855, MJ571, MK775, TE576
T : V6810*, V7066*, MA568
U : P7444, R6833, AB845, AR511, BS464, MJ840, ML259, SL650
V : P8338, V6885*, V7028*, Z3660*, AR548, EP559, MH940, MJ751, MK912, ML179, TE577
W : P3268*, P7540, P8347, V6938, W3445, AA757, BL282, BL852, MA815, MB763, MH315, MJ572, ML233, TE515
X : V6926*, BL340, BL529, BL892, MH356, MK580, ML197, SL527, TE527
Y : P8379, V7468*, LZ920, MH758, MJ783, MK670, ML171, ML212
Z : AR550, AR614, BL487, BL666, MH357, MH367, MH527, MK244, ML367

*Hurricane

SQUADRON BASES, UNITED KINGDOM AND CONTINENTAL EUROPE

Duxford [1]	29.08.40 - 26.09.40	Church Stanton [13]	10.10.42 - 20.02.43
Speke [2]	26.09.40 - 03.03.41	Warmwell [10]	20.02.43 - 14.03.43
Valley [3]	03.03.41 - 25.04.41	Church Stanton [13]	14.03.43 - 24.06.43
Jurby [4]	25.04.41 - 29.05.41	Skeabrae [14]	24.06.43 - 21.09.43
Kenley [5]	29.05.41 - 20.07.41	Ibsley [15]	21.09.43 - 02.12.43
Martlesham Heath [6]	20.07.41 - 19.08.41	Llanbedr [16]	02.12.43 - 18.12.43
Ayr [7]	19.08.41 - 01.01.42	Ibsley [15]	18.12.43 - 19.02.44
Fairwood Common [8]	01.01.42 - 24.01.42	Mendlesham [17]*	19.02.44 - 23.02.44
Angle [9]	24.01.42 - 18.04.42	Southend [18]*	23.02.44 - 03.03.44
Fairwood Common [8]	18.04.42 - 20.04.42	Mendlesham [17]*	03.03.44 - 04.04.44
Warmwell [10]	20.04.42 - 24.04.42	Appledram [19]*	04.04.44 - 22.06.44
Fairwood Common [8]	24.04.42 - 02.05.42	Tangmere [20]*	22.06.44 - 28.06.44
Harrowbeer [11]	02.05.42 - 19.05.42	B10/Plumetôt**[21]*	28.06.44 - 29.06.44
Warmwell [10]	19.05.42 - 31.05.42	Tangmere [20]	29.06.44 - 04.07.44
Harrowbeer [11]	31.05.42 - 01.07.42	Lympne [22]	04.07.44 - 11.07.45
Redhill [12]	01.07.42 - 08.07.42	Coltishall [23]	11.07.44 - 27.08.44
Harrowbeer [11]	08.07.42 - 16.08.42	North Weald [24]	27.08.44 - 03.10.44
Redhill [12]	16.08.42 - 20.08.42	Bradwell Bay [25]	03.10.44 - 27.02.45
Harrowbeer [11]	20.08.42 - 10.10.42	Manston [26]	27.02.45 - 07.08.45

On its way to Prague the unit broke its journey at Hildesheim (R-16), near Hannover, on 07.08.45 and did not continue on to Prague until 13.08.45
* 2 TAF
**France

Last leg to Czechoslovakia was the trip from Hildesheim to Prague-Ruzyne where they arrived on 13.08.45. (A. Thomas)

OPERATIONAL DIARY - NUMBER OF SORTIES

DATE	NUMBER						
		02.12.40	2	15.03.41	10	07.05.41	18
		03.12.40	3	16.03.41	8	08.05.41	7
04.10.40	6	04.12.40	6	19.03.41	2	09.05.41	23
05.10.40	3	05.12.40	6	24.03.41	4	10.05.41	2
07.10.40	3	06.12.40	3	31.03.41	4	11.05.41	9
08.10.40	6	07.12.40	7	*Total for the month : 28*		12.05.41	5
09.10.40	9	08.12.40	6			13.05.41	10
11.10.40	12	10.12.40	9			14.05.41	12
12.10.40	8	11.12.40	4	01.04.41	6	15.05.41	11
13.10.40	15	12.12.40	13	02.04.41	2	16.05.41	5
15.10.40	6	14.12.40	4	03.04.41	2	18.05.41	2
16.10.40	3	15.12.40	7	04.04.41	5	19.05.41	5
20.10.40	2	16.12.40	7	05.04.41	5	20.05.41	7
21.10.40	10	17.12.40	14	06.04.41	11	22.05.41	2
22.10.40	2	18.12.40	12	07.04.41	20	24.05.41	14
23.10.40	4	19.12.40	3	08.04.41	4	25.05.41	2
24.10.40	6	20.12.40	10	09.04.41	1	27.05.41	8
27.10.40	3	21.12.40	4	10.04.41	27	28.05.41	6
28.10.40	9	22.12.40	13	11.04.41	11	*Total for the month : 243*	
29.10.40	2	23.12.40	3	12.04.41	27		
30.10.40	6	24.12.40	9	13.04.41	12	04.06.41	5
Total for the month : 115		26.12.40	4	14.04.41	2	06.06.41	7
		27.12.40	7	15.04.41	6	07.06.41	14
		29.12.40	7	16.04.41	13	09.06.41	20
01.11.40	12	30.12.40	6	17.04.41	3	11.06.41	20
05.11.40	3	*Total for the month : 169*		19.04.41	9	13.06.41	26
07.11.40	12			20.04.41	24	14.06.41	14
08.11.40	6	01.01.41	2	21.04.41	8	15.06.41	20
09.11.40	3	02.01.41	2	22.04.41	4	16.06.41	4
11.11.40	6	03.01.41	3	23.04.41	8	17.06.41	23
13.11.40	6	04.01.41	3	24.04.41	17	18.06.41	12
14.11.40	9	05.01.41	6	25.04.41	24	19.06.41	11
15.11.40	3	08.01.41	36	26.04.41	29	21.06.41	36
16.11.40	12	09.01.41	25	27.04.41	19	22.06.41	24
18.11.40	4	10.01.41	20	28.04.41	20	23.06.41	24
20.11.40	3	11.01.41	6	29.04.41	7	24.06.41	12
21.11.40	3	12.01.41	6	30.04.41	38	25.06.41	26
22.11.40	6	13.01.41	3	*Total for the month : 364*		26.06.41	12
23.11.40	3	15.01.41	5			27.06.41	10
24.11.40	3	17.01.41	5			28.06.41	16
26.11.40	9	21.01.41	2	01.05.41	15	29.06.41	24
27.11.40	3	24.01.41	6	02.05.41	13	30.06.41	12
28.11.40	6	*Total for the month : 130*		03.05.41	18	*Total for the month : 372*	
29.11.40	12			04.05.41	3		
30.11.40	12	07.02.41	4	05.05.41	18	01.07.41	15
Total for the month : 136		*Total for the month : 4*		06.05.41	28	02.07.41	22

Date		Date		Date		Date	
03.07.41	22	01.09.41	6	03.01.42	7	01.03.42	12
04.07.41	13	02.09.41	10	04.01.42	21	02.03.42	2
05.07.41	12	03.09.41	1	05.01.42	15	04.03.42	12
06.07.41	11	06.09.41	6	06.01.42	16	05.03.42	20
07.07.41	23	07.09.41	1	07.01.42	22	07.03.42	18
08.07.41	25	09.09.41	6	08.01.42	18	08.03.42	22
09.07.41	11	10.09.41	1	09.01.42	15	09.03.42	8
10.07.41	11	14.09.41	1	10.01.42	14	10.03.42	25
11.07.41	11	16.09.41	2	11.01.42	19	13.03.42	2
12.07.41	35	28.09.41	2	12.01.42	9	14.03.42	18
13.07.41	2	29.09.41	2	13.01.42	11	15.03.42	2
14.07.41	12	*Total for the month* : **38**		18.01.42	17	18.03.42	2
18.07.41	9			21.01.42	2	19.03.42	12
19.07.41	13			24.01.42	8	20.03.42	20
20.07.41	2	01.10.41	2	25.01.42	22	21.03.42	21
21.07.41	34	02.10.41	2	26.01.42	16	22.03.42	26
22.07.41	28	03.10.41	4	28.01.42	28	23.03.42	14
23.07.41	40	19.10.41	2	29.01.42	4	24.03.42	11
24.07.41	30	21.10.41	2	30.01.42	6	25.03.42	28
25.07.41	22	22.10.41	2	31.01.42	32	26.03.42	20
26.07.41	12	23.10.41	2	*Total for the month* : **302**		27.03.42	10
27.07.41	4	24.10.41	4			28.03.42	8
28.07.41	12	25.10.41	1			29.03.42	12
29.07.41	4	27.10.41	2	01.02.42	4	*Total for the month* : **325**	
30.07.41	6	29.10.41	2	02.02.42	20		
31.07.41	12	*Total for the month* : **25**		03.02.42	24	01.04.42	2
Total for the month : **453**				04.02.42	8	02.04.42	14
				05.02.42	10	03.04.42	16
		02.11.41	2	06.02.42	2	04.04.42	14
01.08.41	14	03.11.41	6	07.02.42	8	05.04.42	6
02.08.41	2	05.11.41	2	08.02.42	34	08.04.42	14
03.08.41	20	06.11.41	2	09.02.42	6	10.04.42	22
04.08.41	6	08.11.41	2	10.02.42	39	11.04.42	18
05.08.41	44	09.11.41	2	11.02.42	18	12.04.42	34
06.08.41	24	12.11.41	1	12.02.42	10	13.04.42	22
07.08.41	27	18.11.41	2	13.02.42	16	14.04.42	8
08.08.41	44	19.11.41	2	14.02.42	16	15.04.42	26
09.08.41	14	21.11.41	6	15.02.42	8	16.04.42	38
10.08.41	24	22.11.41	2	16.02.42	22	17.04.42	20
11.08.41	18	23.11.41	2	17.02.42	21	18.04.42	4
12.08.41	45	24.11.41	2	18.02.42	7	20.04.42	11
14.08.41	41	25.11.41	2	19.02.42	3	22.04.42	11
16.08.41	16	28.11.41	2	20.02.42	2	24.04.42	16
17.08.41	24	29.11.41	2	21.02.42	16	25.04.42	22
18.08.41	16	*Total for the month* : **39**		22.02.42	3	26.04.42	26
24.08.41	2			23.02.42	17	27.04.42	4
25.08.41	4			24.02.42	4	28.04.42	4
28.08.41	2	05.12.41	4	25.02.42	6	30.04.42	22
29.08.41	2	11.12.41	2	26.02.42	14	*Total for the month* : **374**	
30.08.41	10	12.12.41	2	27.02.42	6		
31.08.41	2	31.12.41	6	28.02.42	15	01.05.42	6
Total for the month : **401**		*Total for the month* : **14**		*Total for the month* : **359**		02.05.42	14

03.05.42	6	17.07.42	8	11.09.42	10	24.11.42	4
04.05.42	12	18.07.42	28	12.09.42	2	30.11.42	6
05.05.42	18	19.07.42	14	13.09.42	18	*Total for the month* : **178**	
06.05.42	26	20.07.42	8	14.09.42	2		
07.05.42	36	21.07.42	24	15.09.42	19		
08.05.42	24	22.07.42	18	16.09.42	14	04.12.42	4
09.05.42	16	23.07.42	32	17.09.42	6	06.12.42	12
10.05.42	10	24.07.42	16	18.09.42	20	07.12.42	4
11.05.42	4	25.07.42	10	19.09.42	20	09.12.42	2
27.05.42	12	26.07.42	14	21.09.42	12	11.12.42	4
29.05.42	13	28.07.42	14	22.09.42	2	12.12.42	14
Total for the month : **197**		29.07.42	2	25.09.42	8	14.12.42	6
		30.07.42	26	30.09.42	22	15.12.42	8
		31.07.42	34	*Total for the month* : **318**		17.12.42	2
01.06.42	13	*Total for the month* : **358**				19.12.42	2
02.06.42	16					20.12.42	20
03.06.42	18			01.10.42	22	23.12.41	18
04.06.42	18	02.08.42	2	02.10.42	2	24.12.42	2
05.06.42	20	03.08.42	18	03.10.42	4	29.12.42	2
06.06.42	16	04.08.42	6	06.10.42	2	30.12.42	10
07.06.42	14	05.08.42	6	09.10.42	17	31.12.42	14
09.06.42	4	06.08.42	26	11.10.42	12	*Total for the month* : **124**	
10.06.42	24	08.08.42	6	13.10.42	12		
11.06.42	6	09.08.42	24	14.10.42	14		
14.06.42	16	11.08.42	27	15.10.42	20	02.01.43	12
15.06.42	2	12.08.42	24	16.10.42	14	03.01.43	25
16.06.42	31	13.08.42	28	19.10.42	2	06.01.43	6
17.06.42	10	14.08.42	10	21.10.42	12	07.01.43	2
19.06.42	10	16.08.42	6	22.10.42	4	08.01.43	8
20.10.42	10	17.08.42	4	25.10.42	6	10.01.43	6
21.06.42	4	18.08.42	12	26.10.42	6	11.01.43	6
22.06.42	14	19.08.42	35	27.10.42	16	13.01.43	4
23.06.42	14	23.08.42	22	28.10.42	12	15.01.43	12
24.03.42	24	24.08.42	12	*Total for the month* : **177**		18.01.43	6
25.03.42	10	26.08.42	10			21.01.43	14
26.06.42	14	27.08.42	16			23.01.43	18
27.06.42	8	28.08.42	6	02.11.42	6	24.01.43	4
28.06.42	17	29.08.42	11	03.11.42	16	25.01.43	4
29.06.42	10	31.08.42	6	06.11.42	6	26.01.43	13
30.06.42	11	*Total for the month* : **317**		07.11.42	19	27.01.43	12
Total for the month : **341**				08.11.42	8	29.01.43	10
				09.11.42	2	30.01.43	2
		01.09.42	2	10.11.42	4	*Total for the month* : **164**	
08.07.42	10	02.09.42	10	11.11.42	18		
09.07.42	4	03.09.42	10	13.11.42	4		
10.07.42	14	04.09.42	22	14.11.42	25	02.02.43	6
11.07.42	10	05.09.42	14	16.11.42	6	03.02.43	4
12.07.42	34	06.09.42	16	17.11.42	12	04.02.43	6
13.07.42	4	07.09.42	14	18.11.42	12	05.02.43	6
14.07.42	14	08.09.42	30	21.11.42	6	07.02.43	20
15.07.42	4	09.09.42	16	22.11.42	12	08.02.43	2
16.07.42	16	10.09.42	29	23.11.42	12	09.02.43	4

11.02.43	4	16.04.43	23	23.06.43	12	27.08.43	8
13.02.43	17	18.04.43	18	27.06.43	2	28.08.43	10
15.02.43	10	19.04.43	14	*Total for the month* : **157**		29.08.43	2
16.02.43	14	20.04.43	20			30.08.43	2
17.02.43	10	21.04.43	8			*Total for the month* : **121**	
18.02.43	6	23.04.43	2	01.07.43	4		
19.02.43	16	24.04.43	8	04.07.43	4		
26.02.43	14	25.04.43	10	05.07.43	3	02.09.43	10
27.02.43	20	26.04.43	8	07.07.43	2	03.09.43	10
28.02.43	12	27.04.43	11	08.07.43	2	04.09.43	4
Total for the month : **171**		28.04.43	2	09.07.43	4	05.09.43	6
		30.04.43	4	11.07.43	2	06.09.43	7
		Total for the month : **315**		12.07.43	4	07.09.43	6
01.03.43	8			13.07.43	2	08.09.43	17
03.03.43	14			14.07.43	4	09.09.43	4
04.03.43	12	01.05.43	24	16.07.43	6	10.09.43	6
07.03.43	18	02.05.43	24	17.07.43	6	12.09.43	4
08.03.43	18	04.05.43	12	18.07.43	2	15.09.43	10
09.03.43	20	05.05.43	8	19.07.43	26	16.09.43	4
10.03.43	16	06.05.43	10	20.07.43	4	17.09.43	8
11.03.43	14	07.05.43	14	21.07.43	2	18.09.43	8
12.03.43	18	09.05.43	2	22.07.43	6	19.09.43	2
13.03.43	14	11.05.43	2	23.07.43	4	22.09.43	10
14.03.43	11	13.05.43	6	26.07.43	2	23.09.43	20
15.03.43	18	14.05.43	26	27.07.43	10	24.09.43	21
16.03.43	20	15.05.43	4	28.07.43	12	26.09.43	4
19.03.43	10	16.05.43	24	29.07.43	15	27.09.43	22
20.03.43	14	17.05.43	30	30.07.43	2	*Total for the month* : **183**	
21.03.43	10	18.05.43	14	*Total for the month* : **128**			
23.03.43	2	19.05.43	11				
24.03.43	4	23.05.43	16			02.10.43	14
26.03.43	12	25.05.43	34	03.08.43	2	03.10.43	11
28.03.43	14	27.05.43	2	04.08.43	10	04.10.43	10
29.03.43	10	28.05.43	34	06.08.43	4	07.10.43	10
30.03.43	14	29.05.43	23	07.08.43	6	08.10.43	11
31.03.43	4	30.05.43	18	08.08.43	2	09.10.43	10
Total for the month : **295**		31.05.43	12	09.08.43	4	14.10.43	2
		Total for the month : **350**		10.08.43	4	15.10.43	2
				11.08.43	2	17.10.43	16
03.04.43	13			12.08.43	2	20.10.43	2
04.04.43	22	02.06.43	4	13.08.43	2	22.10.43	12
05.04.43	20	03.06.43	6	14.08.43	2	24.10.43	20
06.04.43	14	05.06.43	6	15.08.43	8	25.10.43	11
07.04.43	6	06.06.43	14	16.08.43	2	26.10.43	6
08.04.43	11	07.06.43	16	17.08.43	8	28.10.43	11
09.04.43	20	12.06.43	24	19.08.43	6	29.10.43	4
10.04.43	10	13.03.43	11	20.08.43	4	30.10.43	22
11.04.43	4	14.06.43	8	22.08.43	2	*Total for the month* : **174**	
12.04.43	10	16.06.43	30	23.08.43	4		
13.04.43	20	17.06.43	8	24.08.43	4		
14.04.43	19	20.06.43	4	25.08.43	6	01.11.43	2
15.04.43	18	22.06.43	12	26.08.43	15	03.11.43	12

Date	No.	Date	No.	Date	No.	Date	No.
05.11.43	16	04.03.44	12	08.06.44	38	24.08.44	12
07.11.43	13	15.03.44	11	10.06.44	49	25.08.44	4
08.11.43	6	23.03.44	25	11.06.44	38	26.08.44	12
10.11.43	10	26.03.44	12	12.06.44	37	27.08.44	12
11.11.43	14	27.03.44	12	13.06.44	13	28.08.44	12
14.11.43	8	28.03.44	12	14.06.44	24	30.08.44	12
17.11.43	4	*Total for the month : 84*		15.06.44	25	31.08.44	12
24.11.43	8			16.06.44	25	*Total for the month : 160*	
25.11.43	16			17.06.44	28		
26.11.43	23	08.04.44	12	18.06.44	25		
28.11.43	4	12.04.44	12	19.06.44	25	01.09.44	12
29.11.43	8	13.04.44	26	20.06.44	24	03.09.44	12
Total for the month : 144		15.04.44	6	21.06.44	13	05.09.44	12
		17.04.44	8	22.06.44	36	06.09.44	12
		18.04.44	13	23.06.44	37	09.09.44	23
01.12.43	12	19.04.44	24	24.06.44	12	10.09.44	12
20.12.43	6	20.04.44	25	25.06.44	12	11.09.44	12
21.12.43	12	21.04.44	11	27.06.44	12	12.09.44	22
22.12.43	13	23.04.44	24	28.06.44	22	13.09.44	23
23.12.43	10	24.04.44	13	29.06.44	12	14.09.44	12
24.12.43	10	*Total for the month : 174*		30.06.44	15	16.09.44	16
27.12.43	2			*Total for the month : 648*		17.09.44	25
30.12.43	11					18.09.44	12
31.12.43	20	02.05.44	12			19.09.44	6
Total for the month : 96		03.05.44	24	01.07.44	12	20.09.44	13
		04.05.44	29	02.07.44	12	23.09.44	12
		07.05.44	25	04.07.44	22	26.09.44	12
		08.05.44	12	05.07.44	20	27.09.44	24
01.01.44	2	09.05.44	13	06.07.44	24	30.09.44	12
02.01.44	8	10.05.44	24	07.07.44	32	*Total for the month : 284*	
04.01.44	12	11.05.44	26	08.07.44	4		
05.01.44	12	12.05.44	24	09.07.44	11		
06.01.44	8	13.05.44	26	10.07.44	11	06.10.44	12
07.01.44	14	15.05.44	8	16.07.44	23	07.10.44	12
09.01.44	8	19.05.44	7	20.07.44	4	11.10.44	12
14.01.44	12	20.05.44	23	23.07.44	4	12.10.44	12
21.01.44	16	21.05.44	12	26.07.44	16	14.10.44	12
23.01.44	12	22.05.44	12	*Total for the month : 195*		16.10.44	11
26.01.44	12	24.05.44	21			18.10.44	12
29.01.44	11	25.05.44	12			21.10.44	11
Total for the month : 127		27.05.44	24	03.08.44	2	23.10.44	4
		28.05.44	2	08.08.44	6	25.10.44	12
		29.05.44	12	09.08.44	4	28.10.44	24
04.02.44	8	30.05.44	24	11.08.44	8	29.10.44	11
07.02.44	9	*Total for the month : 372*		12.08.44	6	30.10.44	12
08.02.44	12			14.08.44	14	*Total for the month : 157*	
09.02.44	12			15.08.44	12		
10.02.44	12	02.06.44	13	16.08.44	12		
11.02.44	12	03.06.44	2	17.08.44	4	01.11.44	12
12.02.44	6	05.06.44	12	18.08.44	12	04.11.44	12
15.02.44	18	06.06.44	50	22.08.44	2	06.11.44	12
Total for the month : 89		07.06.44	49	23.08.44	2	08.11.44	12

09.11.44	9	28.01.45	12	12.03.45	12	18.04.45	9
16.11.44	13	*Total for the month* : **35**		13.03.45	13	19.04.45	8
18.11.44	11			14.03.45	12	22.04.45	2
20.11.44	12			15.03.45	12	*Total for the month* : **77**	
21.11.44	12	01.02.45	12	17.03.45	11		
26.11.44	13	03.02.45	11	19.03.45	12		
27.11.44	11	06.02.45	12	20.03.45	12	**GRAND TOTAL** : **11,013**	
29.11.44	11	07.02.45	11	21.03.45	12		
30.11.44	12	08.02.45	11	22.03.45	11	Extracted from ORB	
Total for the month : **152**		10.02.45	11	23.03.45	12	AIR27/1691-1696.	
		14.02.45	13	24.03.45	11		
04.12.44	12	21.02.45	12	25.03.45	12		
05.12.44	12	22.02.45	10	30.03.45	2		
08.12.44	12	23.02.45	9	31.03.45	12		
11.12.44	12	24.02.45	11	*Total for the month* : **215**			
15.12.44	12	27.02.45	12				
23.12.44	12	28.02.45	2				
24.12.44	12	*Total for the month* : **137**					
29.12.44	12			03.04.45	12		
31.12.44	12			04.04.45	11		
Total for the month : **108**		01.03.45	10	06.04.45	2		
		02.03.45	22	09.04.45	10		
		08.03.45	2	11.04.45	10		
05.01.45	11	09.03.45	12	13.04.45	11		
17.01.45	12	11.03.45	13	14.04.45	2		

RAF Penrhos during the winter of 1940 - 1941. Leading Aircraftman T. Zrnik is assisting the pilot, Sergeant F. Kruta, to fasten his seat belts for an immediate take off in Hurricane P3612/DU-N. Note the blanked off gun port as this Hurricane I, like all others of this mark, was armed with four machine guns in each wing and not five. (via Andrew Thomas).

Claim list of probable (P) and confirmed (C) kills

Date	Pilot	Type	Serial	Number	Statute
		HURRICANE I			
08.10.40	F/L D.E. Gillam	Ju88	P2575/R	0.333	C
	Sgt J. Stehlik		L1807	0.333	C
	P/O A. Vasatko		L1926/J	0.333	C

No.312 Squadron's first victory, Ju88A-1 (Wnr.4086) of 2./KGr806 coded M7+DK, was shot down on 08.10.40. (Jiri Rajlich)

Date	Pilot	Type	Serial	Number	Statute
14.03.41	F/L A.M. Dawbarn	Ju88	?	0.5	C
	Sgt J. Stehlik		V6926/X	0.5	C
		HURRICANE II			
18.06.41	Sgt O. Kucera	Bf109	Z3437/K	1	P
03.07.41	Sgt O. Kucera	Bf109	Z3314/J	1	C
05.07.41	F/Sgt V. Smolik	Bf109	Z3592	1	P
08.07.41	F/Sgt V. Smolik	Bf109	Z3467/E	1	C
09.07.41	Sgt A. Zavoral	Bf109	Z3181	1	C
	F/Sgt O. Kucera	Bf109	Z3314/J	1	C
	F/L A. Vasatko	Bf109	Z3660/W	1	P
10.07.41	F/Sgt J. Stehlik	Bf109	Z3221/L	1	P
		SPITFIRE V			
16.02.42	P/O O. Kucera	Ju88	BL381/L	1	C

21.03.42	F/L B. Dvorak	Ju88	AD553/D	0.5	C
	Sgt J. Dobrovolny		BL381/L	0.5	C
03.06.42	F/O F. Perina	FW190	AD572/C	1	C
19.08.42	F/Sgt T. Motycka	FW190	AA970	1	P
	Sgt V. Ruprecht	FW190	EP518/N	1	P
	Sgt M. Liskutin	Do215	EP660/O [1]	0.5	C
	F/O J. Keprt	Do215	EP432/R	1	C
04.04.43	F/Sgt S. Tocauer	FW190	EE680	1	P
27.08.43	F/L K. Kasal	Ju88	AA911	0.5	C
	F/O K. Posta		W3253	0.5	C

SPITFIRE IX

23.03.44	F/O L. Svetlik	FW190	MJ931	1	C
08.06.44	W/C J. Cermak	FW190	MK244	1	C
	Sgt V. Angetter	FW190	MK449/R	1	C
10.06.44	F/Sgt J. Konvicka	Bf109	MJ940 [2]	1	P

[1] Shared with a pilot of No.131 Sqn
[2] By collision

Total : 22.5

Aircraft damaged : 13

The tail of the Ju 88 shot down on 08.10.44 became the Squadron's trophy and it is proudly shown by Sergeant J. Stehlik (left) and Pilot Officer A. Vasatko (right). (Jiri Rajlich)

Aircraft Lost on Operations

Date	Pilot	Cause	Serial	Mark	Fate
		HURRICANE			
15.10.40	F/L H.A.G. Comerford	3	V6542	I	-
	P/O T. Vybiral	3	V6811	I	-
10.04.41	F/L A.A.M. Dawbarn	1	V7066/T	I	†
03.05.41	Sgt J. Mensik	3	P3983/Q	I	-
06.05.41	Sgt B. Votruba	3	V6921/R	I	†
23.06.41	F/O T. Kruml	3	Z3436 **[1]**	IIB	-
08.07.41	Sgt J. Mensik	1	Z3327	IIB	Eva.
09.07.41	Sgt J. Truhlar	1	Z3023	IIB	PoW
		SPITFIRE			
24.01.42	Sgt M. Liskutin	3	R6883/U	VA	-
27.04.42	F/L R. Rohacek	3	AD553/E	VB	†
02.05.42	P/O J. Janeba	3	BL470/J	VB	†
	Sgt F. Vaculik	3	BL231/B	VB	-
03.06.42	F/L B. Dvorak	1	BL340/X	VB	PoW
	F/O I. Tonder	1	BL626/I	VB	PoW
29.06.42	F/L A. Liska	3	AB172/O	VB	-
06.01.43	F/Sgt M. Liskutin	3	AR548/V	VB	-
14.05.43	F/O J. Novak	2	EP539/C	VB	†
25.10.43	F/O J. Stastny	2	AB372/B	VB	†
19.04.44	F/L B. Budil	1	MK248/R	IX	PoW
21.05.44	W/O R. Ossendorf	2	MJ907/A	IX	Eva.
10.06.44	Sgt J. Konvicka	1	MJ940/J **[1]**	IX	-
11.06.44	F/L V. Smolik	3	MK580/X	IX	-
	F/L F. Truhlar	3	MJ499/R	IX	-
	Sgt V. Nosek	3	MJ840/L	IX	†
11.08.44	F/Sgt A. Pristupa	3	ML240/H	IX	PoW
25.08.44	W/O V. Ruprecht	3	ML245/R	IX	†
28.08.44	F/L K. Posta	3	MK691	IX	-
	F/Sgt J. Konvicka	3	ML154	IX	-
03.09.44	F/L O. Smik	2	ML296/N	IX	Eva.
18.09.44	F/Sgt A. Ocelka	2	MK682/C	IX	PoW
08.12.44	F/Sgt J. Skrinar	3	AB505/Q	IX	-
	Sgt J. Vanko	3	MH357/Z	IX	†
31.12.44	F/L Z. Donda	3	MH354/J	IX	†
01.02.45	2nd Lt A.C. Gaydos	3	BS458/F	IX	-

[1] By collision.

Total : 34

1 *Enemy aircraft*
2 *Flak*
3 *Other causes*

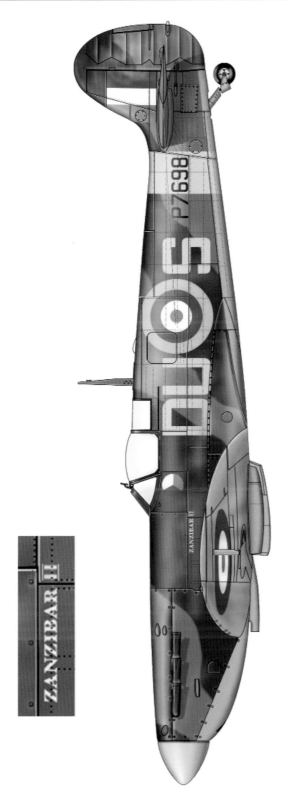

Supermarine Spitfire Mk.IIA P7698 "Zanzibar II", No.312 (Czechoslovak) Squadron, Ayr, December 1941.
This mark was used for a short time by the Squadron and for training purpose only.
Sergeants T. Motycka and J. Kucera were among the pilots who flew this aircraft the most.

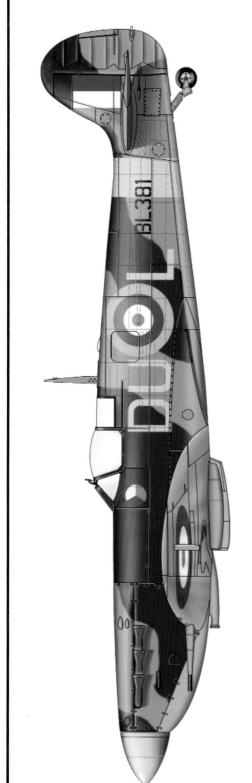

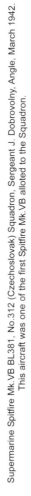

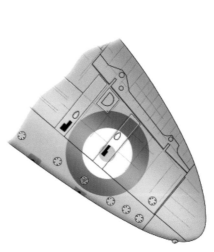

Supermarine Spitfire Mk.VB BL381, No.312 (Czechoslovak) Squadron, Sergeant J. Dobrovolny, Angle, March 1942. This aircraft was one of the first Spitfire Mk.VB alloted to the Squadron.

Aircraft Lost by Accident

Date	Pilot	Duty	Serial	Mark	Fate
		Hurricane			
10.09.40	Sgt K. Keprt	Training flight	L1644	I	-
10.10.40	Sgt O. Hanzlicek	Training flight	L1547	I	†
13.02.41	F/O J. Bartos	Practice	V6885/V	I	†
22.02.41	Sgt F. Kruta	Practice	P3612/N	I	-
26.09.41	F/O T. Vybiral	Practice. Mid-air coll.	Z3091	II	-
		Spitfire			
25.10.41	F/O F. Hekl	Practice	P7460/W	II	†
19.12.41	F/Sgt V. Smolik	Practice. Mid-air coll.	AD539	VB	-
	Sgt J. Kucera	Practice. Mid-air coll.	BL293	VB	†
02.05.42	F/L V. Kaslik	Practice	BL381/L	VB	-
11.03.44	Sgt A. Ocelka	Practice	MJ637/B	IX	-
15.05.44	W/O A. Prvonic	Collision on the ground	MK608/D	IX	†
09.02.45	F/Sgt O. Samberger	Practice	LZ951/D	IX	†
	F/O A. Zalesky	Practice	BS433/G	IX	†

Total : 13

The remains of Sgt F. Kruta's Hurricane after his accident of 22.02.41. He escaped unhurt. (Andrew Thomas)

†

ROLL OF HONOUR-AIRCREW

Name	Service No	Rank	Age	Origin	Date	Serial
BARTOS, J.	RAF 83220	F/O	29	(cz)/RAF	13.02.41	V6885
DAWBARN, A.A.M.	RAF 40213	F/L	n/a	RAF	10.04.41	V7066
DONDA, Z.	RAF 131536	F/L	23	(cz)/RAF	31.12.44	MH354
HANZLICEK, O.	RAF 787697	Sgt	29	(cz)/RAF	10.10.40	L1547
HEKL, F.	RAF 87619	F/O	26	(cz)/RAF	25.10.41	P7540
JANEBA, J.	RAF 113884	P/O	27	(cz)/RAF	02.05.42	BL231
KUCERA, J.	RAF 787665	Sgt	26	(cz)/RAF	19.12.41	BL293
NOSEK, V.	RAF 787647	F/Sgt	28	(cz)/RAF	11.06.44	MJ840
NOVAK, J.	RAF 117370	F/O	27	(cz)/RAF	14.05.43	EP539
PRVONIC, A.	RAF 788090	W/O	29	(cz)/RAF	15.05.44	MK608
ROHACEK, R.	RAF 81910	F/L	27	(cz)/RAF	27.04.42	AD553
RUPRECHT, V.	RAF 787526	W/O	26	(cz)/RAF	25.08.44	ML245
SAMBERGER, O.	RAF 787806	Sgt	28	(cz)/RAF	09.02.45	LZ951
STASTNY, J.	RAF 125415	F/O	30	(cz)/RAF	25.10.43	AB372
VANKO, A.	RAF 788644	Sgt	26	(cz)/RAF	08.12.44	MH527
VOTRUBA, B.	RAF 787435	F/Sgt	27	(cz)/RAF	20.04.41	V6921
ZALESKY, A.	RAF 185292	F/O	28	(cz)/RAF	09.02.45	BS433

Sergeant Otto Hanzlicek in September 1940. He became
No.312 (Czech) Squadron's first war casualty and also its only
loss during the Battle of Britain. (Jiri Rajlich)

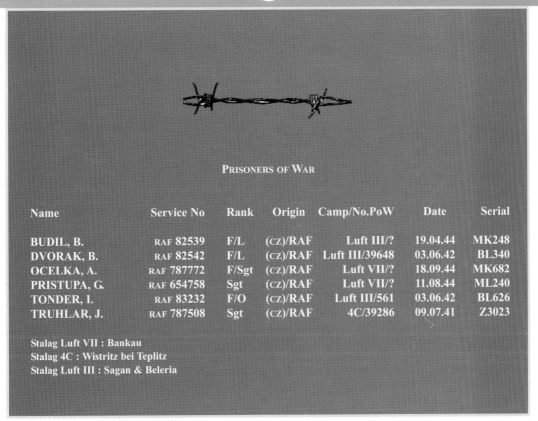

PRISONERS OF WAR

Name	Service No	Rank	Origin	Camp/No.PoW	Date	Serial
BUDIL, B.	RAF 82539	F/L	(CZ)/RAF	Luft III/?	19.04.44	MK248
DVORAK, B.	RAF 82542	F/L	(CZ)/RAF	Luft III/39648	03.06.42	BL340
OCELKA, A.	RAF 787772	F/Sgt	(CZ)/RAF	Luft VII/?	18.09.44	MK682
PRISTUPA, G.	RAF 654758	Sgt	(CZ)/RAF	Luft VII/?	11.08.44	ML240
TONDER, I.	RAF 83232	F/O	(CZ)/RAF	Luft III/561	03.06.42	BL626
TRUHLAR, J.	RAF 787508	Sgt	(CZ)/RAF	4C/39286	09.07.41	Z3023

Stalag Luft VII : Bankau
Stalag 4C : Wistritz bei Teplitz
Stalag Luft III : Sagan & Beleria

Pilots of No.312 (Czech) Squadron during Summer 1941.
Let to right : Sgt Z. Karasek, F/Sgts K. Posta, S. Peroutka, L. Svetlik, V. Smolik, Sgt M. Standera, F/Sgt V. Slouf, P/O I. Tonder (who became a PoW one year later), F/Sgts O. Kucera, F. Sticka and J. Sodek. They posing in front Hurricane IIB Z3660/DU-V which was the usual mount of Squadron Leader A. Vasatko. (via Andrew Thomas)

Squadron founder members, Duxford in September 1940.
Front row L-R: P/O F.S. Lamping (Adjutant), F/L J. Duda, S/L J. Ambrus, S/L F.H. Tyson, F/L D.E. Gillam, F/L A. Hlobil, P/O G.McK. Philips (Intelligence Officer).
Middle row : P/O A. Brejcha, P/O J. Klan, P/O J. Cermak, P/O S. Krejcik (Technical Officer), P/O J. Jaske, P/O A. Vasatko, P/O J. Bartos, P/O B. Dvorak, P/O T. Vybiral, P/O T. Kruml, P/O A. Vrana, P/O J. Burger, P/O A. Navratil.
Back row : Sgt V. Slouf, Sgt J. Keprt, Sgt K. Posta, Sgt B. Votruba, Sgt J. Stehlik, Sgt J. Truhlar, Sgt F. Chabera, Sgt J. Janeba, Sgt V. Smolik and Sgt S. Peroutka.
Most were still wearing French uniforms. (Jiri Rajlich)

SQUADRON ROSTER

NAME	RANK[1]	STATUS

*Flight Leader, ** Squadron Leader, ***Flight Leader/Squadron Leader*

@ *Pilots at the Squadron in August 1945.*

(†) *Pilots killed serving with Squadron.*

AMBRUS, Jan · S/L · (CZ)/RAF
9-40/12-40[2] · RAF No.81883

Slovak[3]. Posted from No.6 OTU. Pre-war CzAF fighter pilot with Air Regiment 6[4]. With *Armée de l'Air* 1940 serving in CIC Chartres before escaping to the UK.

[1] When first posted.
[2] Time passed with the Squadron (Month-Year). Unless stated, every pilot is presumed to have survived the War.
[3] Unless stated, all the pilots are Czech.
[4] An overview of the pre-war CzAF is available in the No.310 (Czechoslovak) Squadron book published in this series.
[5] When a pilot has two service numbers, the first refers to Non-Commissioned Officers (NCO), the second to Officers.

Posted to No.310 (Czech) Sqn as reserve pilot, but did not fly, having to be trained on Hurricane and posted to No.6 OTU as such. Withdrawn from operational duty due of his age, 41 in 1940. Member of Czechoslovak Military mission, later Czechoslovak Military and Air Attaché in Canada until the end of the war. After the war he remained with the new CzAF. He was promoted to the rank Brigadier General but after Communist coup he emigrated and settled in the USA. He was the only Slovak fighter pilot of the Battle of Britain.

ANGETTER, Vit · Sgt · (CZ)/RAF
5-44/8-45 @ · RAF No.787119

Posted from No.84 GSU. After the war he flew as co-pilot at company CSA. In March 1950 he took part in the escape of former RAF pilots. One confirmed victory, No.312 Sqn, Europe, 1944.

F/Sgt : 9-44, W/O : 2-45, P/O : 6-45

J. AMBRUS

BACHUREK, Svatopluk   P/O   (CZ)/RAF
10-40/7-41   RAF No.82536
Pre-war CzAF pilot, serving with Air Regiment 6. Posted to No.245 Sqn, but subsequently posted to No.32 Sqn (September - November 1941) and No.615 Sqn remaining three weeks only in November 1941. Subsequently posted to No.124 Sqn.
†25.04.42, Spitfire VB W3332, No.124 Sqn, France.

B. BUDIL

BARTOS, Frantisek   Sgt   (CZ)/RAF
12-44/1-45   RAF No.787052
Posted from No.57 OTU. No details available.
F/Sgt : 1-45

BARTOS, Jindrich   P/O   (CZ)/RAF
9-40/2-41 (†)   RAF No.83220
Czech born in Russia. Pre-war CzAF pilot serving with Air Regiment 2. In 1939 he escaped to France via Poland. Joined the *Armée de l' Air* and posted on 17.05.40 to GC I/3 flying Dewoitine 520s. On 03.06.40, he claimed a probable destroyed He111 but was himself was shot down and wounded. After the fall of France escaped to the United Kingdom. Killed during a mock fight.
F/O : 1-41

BEDNAR, Josef   Sgt   (CZ)/RAF
6-44/8-45 @   RAF No.787716 [5]
   RAF No.189763
Background unknown. Returned to Czechoslovakia, but after the Communist coup he emigrated and later settled in USA.
F/Sgt : 10-44, W/O : 11-44, P/O : 12-44

BENSON, Niale S.T.   F/O   RAF
9-40/10-40   RAF No.70060
Pre-war RAF Reserve officer recalled on active service in December 1939. Attached from No.11 FTS between 22.09.40 and 05.10.40 to give training to the Czech pilots and returned to his unit. Squadron Leader at the end of war and remained with the RAF until 1957. AFC [31.03.42].

BILEK, Jindrich   Sgt   RAF
5-44/8-45 @   RAF No.787140
Posted from No.84 GSU. No details available.
F/Sgt : 9-44, W/O : 2-45, P/O : 6-45

BUDIL, Bohuslav   F/O   (CZ)/RAF
9-42/4-44   RAF No.82539
Posted from No.51 OTU. Pre-war CzAF pilot, serving with Air Regiment 2. In November 1938 he attended to study on L'*École Nationale Supérieure de l'Aéronautique* (French Aeronautics Academy) in Paris. When the war broke out he joined the *Armée de l' Air* but at non-operational postings. After the fall of

France he escaped to England. At first he served with No.24 Sqn during 1940 - 1941. Shot down by fighters during *Ramrod* 753 and became prisoner of war.
F/L : 11-42

BURGER, Josef   P/O   (CZ)/RAF
9-40/7-41   RAF No.83222
Pre-war CzAF pilot. In 1939 he joined the *Armée de l'Air*, on 18.05.40 he was posted to GC II/5 flying Curtisses. On 05.06.40 he was wounded in action fighting Bf109s. Escaped to the UK. Later GCI duties.
F/O : 1-41

CAP, Karel   W/O   (CZ)/RAF
8-43/8-44   RAF No.787544
Posted for his second tour of operations. When the war broke he joined the *Armée de l' Air*. On 16.11.39 he was posted to ERC 571, which became a few weeks later part of GC III/4 in North Africa. Escaped to England. Later posted to No.245 Sqn until June 1941 when he was posted to No.313 (Czech) Sqn completed his tour in August 1942. Posted out, tour expired.

CERMAK, Jan* **   P/O   (CZ)/RAF
9-40/5-41, 7-41/1-43   RAF No.84666
In 1931 he enlisted to the Czechoslovak Army. In July 1932 was posted to the Observation Flight 13 of Air Regiment 3 as an observer. Next year he entered into the Military Academy being graduated in July 1935. Then he served as pilot with Air Regiments 3 and 1. In June 1939 he escaped to France, via Poland. Enlisted in the *Armée de l' Air* and on 17.05.40 was posted to the Front. He served with GC III/3 flying Moranes and Dewoitines and on 13.06.40 he shared a confirmed victory (He111). After the fall of France escaped to the UK. In May 1941 he was posted to No.313 (Czech) Sqn but returned to No.312 Sqn two months later as A flight leader between 21.07.41 and 30.04.42, replacing J. Jaske. He relinquished the A flight to V. Kaslik on 01.05.42 to become Squadron's CO. Posted out at the end of his tour in January 1943. Subsequently he served at Czechoslovak Air Ministry in London as a liaison Officer at HQ of Fighter Command. Later CO No.134 (Czechoslovak) Airfield. Two confirmed victories, one being shared, with the French, 1940, and No.134 Wing, Normandy, 1944. After the war he was temporary commander of 4th Air Division in Trencin and he commanded 3rd Air Division in Brno. After the

Communist coup he was arrested but due of the lack of evidence, he was released.
F/O : 1-41, F/L : 12-41, S/L : 12-41, W/C : 1-43

CERMAK, Josef   Sgt   (CZ)/RAF
10-43/5-44   RAF No.787363
Posted from No.61 OTU. Pre-war sport pilot. With Czech Depot at Agde in France 1939-40, then fleed to the UK. After completing his pilot training in England posted to No.312 (Czech) Sqn. Posted to No.118 Sqn between May and July 1944, then No.313 (Czech) Sqn July - September 1944, No.310 (Czech) Sqn between September 1944 and August 1945. He was killed in flying accident on 17.12.45 as a crew member of a Si-204 in Czechoslovakia.

CHABERA, Frantisek   Sgt   (CZ)/RAF
9-40/3-41, 8-42/2-44   RAF No.787698
                                               RAF No.115117
Czech born in Germany, but his family moved to the part of Austro-Hungary which later became Czechoslovakia. In October 1930 he enlisted to the Army and sent to the Military Flying School in Prostejov. He was at first a pilot of observation aircraft then bomber and eventually of fighter (Air Regiment 2 & 4). In August 1935, he was sent to the Military Technical & Aeronautical Institute in Prague-Letnany

J. CERMAK

as a test pilot. On 09.06.39 he escaped to France via Poland. Joined the *Armée de l' Air* and on 02.12.39 was posted to GC II/5 flying Curtisses. He claimed his first victory (shared) on 11.05.40, followed by another four confirmed (one being shared) and two probable victories. After the fall of France he retreated to North Africa and subsequently set up to United Kingdom, via Gibraltar. He later went to a night training flight syllabus was posted to No.96 Sqn equiped with Defiants. Remained with it until September and was posted to the Czech flight of No.68 Sqn until May 1942, the end of his tour. Commissioned in December 1941. Then served at Czechoslovak Air Ministry and was posted for his second tour to No.312 Sqn. Discharged from RAF On 01.02.44, being volunteer to serve in Soviet Union with the 1ˢᵗ Czechoslovak Fighter Air Regiment. After the reorganization of the regiment he became the commander of the 1ˢᵗ flight. After the war he became a test pilot at the Military Research Institute. In December 1948 he was arrested and later sentenced for having to attempt to escape from the Country. He spent five years in jail.
F/O : 12-42, F/L : 12-43

E. CIZEK

CHOCHOLIN, Vladislav   P/O   (CZ)/RAF
9-40/9-40   RAF No.81886
Posted from No.310 (Czech) Sqn where he was a founder member in July 1940. Known as "*Chocho*". Pre-war CzAF fighter pilot in Air Regiment 6. With *Armée de l'Air* 1939-1940 before escaping to the UK. Posted back to No.310 Sqn, remaining with it until the end of his first tour in January 1943. Returned to No.310 Sqn for his second tour until his death.
†24.09.43, Spitfire VC AR335, No.310 (Czech) Sqn, France.

CIZEK, Evzen**   S/L   (CZ)/RAF
12-40/5-41   RAF No.85921
Posted from No.1 Sqn. Born in 1904, he enlisted in the Army in 1922 and transferred to the Air Force in 1928, being trained as an observer and later as fighter pilot. In March 1939, he was CO of fighter flight 32. After the occupation of his country he escaped to France via Poland. When the war broke out he joined the *Armée de l' Air* and on 02.12.39, he was posted to GC III/3 (flying Moranes later Dewoitines). Claimed five victories with the French, the first on 11.05.40 when he shot down a Bf109. His last victory was claimed on Dewoitine on 06.06.40. After the fall of France he retreated to North Africa and organised the evacuation of Czechoslovak

pilots to the United Kingdom. In August he sailed to Portugal and subsequently to England by air. He joined the RAF. After retraining at No.6 OTU, he was posted to No.1 Sqn in October 1940 remaining until December. In May 1941 he was transferred to Military Office of President Eduard Benes and in September he was posted to HQ of Fighter Command as a liaison officer of Czechoslovak Air Ministry.
†26.11.42, Warferry GM.1 (ex G-AFKO), Station Flight Northolt, UK.

COMERFORD, Harry A.G.**   F/L   RAF
9-40/11-40   RAF No.24051
Posted from No.6 EFTS. Pre-war RAF pilot who served with Nos.28 Sqn and 31 Sqns in India. In 1934 he went to the Reserve of Officers but was recalled on duty when the war broke out. Posted as A flight commander. Replaced by C.A. Cooke when he left the Squadron on 15.11.40. He resigned his commission in April 1943. AFC [30.09.41].

COOKE, Charles A.*   F/L   RAF
12-40/5-41   RAF No.43634
Posted from No.66 Sqn in was serving with since April 1940. Posted in to take command of A flight, as British double of J. Klan. posted out at the end of his tour in

May 1941, being replaced by J. Jaske on 28.05.41. Another tour with No.264 Sqn as CO between December 1941 and May 1942 when he relinquished his command. Remained with No.264 Sqn until the end of his tour in October 1942. No more operational postings until the end of war. One confirmed victory, No.264 Sqn, Europe, 1942. DFC [No.264 Sqn].
F/L : 12-40

DAWBARN, Alexander A.M.* F/O RAF
12-40/4-41 (†) RAF No.40213
Posted from No.306 (Polish) Sqn, in which he was serving since October, to take charge of B Flight on 01.12.40 succeeding D.E. Gillam. Pre-war RAF officer. Shot down and killed in the combat with Bf110s. Replaced by A. Vasatko. One shared confirmed victory, No.312 Sqn, Europe, 1941.
F/L : 12-40

DOBROVOLNY, Jaroslav Sgt (CZ)/RAF
7-41/3-42, 7-42/4-43 RAF No.788012
Posted from No.52 OTU. Pre-war CzAF pilot serving with Air Regiment 3. Wounded in combat on 21.03.42 returing to the Squadron in July. Posted to No.3 ADF, tour expired. Later commissioned and posted to No.313 (Czech) Sqn in October 1943 for a second tour of operations until the end of war.
F/Sgt : 9-42, W/O : 10-42

DONDA, Zdenek F/L (CZ)/RAF
11-44/12-44 (†) RAF No.131536
Posted from No.57 OTU. Former wireless operator with No.311 (Czechoslovak) Sqn before to be accepted for a pilot course. He passed the fighter pilot training and on 16.11.44 was posted to No 312 squadron as supernumerary Flight Lieutenant. On 31.12.1944 he made a crash landing in Lovendegem and died of wounds.

DUDA, Josef * F/L (CZ)/RAF
9-40/11-40 RAF No.83224
Pre-war regular officer in Artillery switching as Observer in the Air Force in 1928. Then fighter pilot in 1933. In June 1939 he escaped to Poland and subsequently to France. There, he enlisted in the *Armée de l' Air* and after being retrained on French fighters he was posted to GC II/5 flying Curtisses on 18.05.40. Claimed with the French two victories, both being shared. After the fall of

France he escaped to the United Kingdom. Posted to F.P.P. and Maintenance Units and later at Czechoslovak Air Ministry in London. First A Flight leader between 05.09.40 and 30.09.40 pending the arrival of H.A.G. Comerford.

DVORAK, Antonin* P/O (CZ)/RAF
9-42/5-44, 11-44/8-45 @ RAF No.115864
Posted from No.52 OTU for a second tour of operations, having completed the first one with No.501 Sqn between April 1941 and February 1942. After his rest, he was posted to No.312 Sqn for another tour. Posted to No.84 Group Communication Squadron in May 1944. On 01.11.44, he returned to the Squadron as supernumerary Flight Lieutenant and stayed at unit till the end of war. Last A Flight Commander from 17.02.45 onwards, replacing K. Posta.
F/O : 1-43, F/L : 3-44

DVORAK, Bedrich P/O (CZ)/RAF
9-40/6-42, 6-45/8-45 @ RAF No.82542
Posted from OTU. Pre-war CzAF pilot with Air Regiment 2. In June 1939 he escaped to France via Poland. There, he joined the *Armée de l' Air* and in March 1940 he was posted to GC III/7 flying Moranes being wounded in action during the Phoney War

B. DVORAK

(31.03.40). Escaped to the United Kingdom and joined the RAF. On 03.06.42 he was shot down by a FW190. He bailed out into the Channel and was rescued by French fishermen and subsequently became a PoW. He took part to the "Great Escape" on 24.03.44. He was re-captured and he was eventually liberated on 16.04.45 and returned to the Squadron in June 1945.
F/O : 1-41, F/L : 12-41

FIRSOV, Nikola Sgt (CZ)/RAF
5-45/8-45 @   RAF No.788439
Posted from No.57 OTU. Former infantryman with No.11 Czech Infantry Battalion in the Middle East and North Africa. In January 1943 he was sent back to the United Kingdom and enlisted in the RAF.

GAYDOS, Albert C. 2ⁿᵈ Lt USAAF
7-44/4-45   O-10601636
Slovak. Posted from No.313 (Czech) Sqn in which he was serving since October 1944. Son of Slovak emigrants in Canada. First enlisting in the RAF (s/n 654739) and was transferred to the USAAF in January 1944. Posted to 12ᵗʰ Replacement Control Depot, USAAF at the end of his tour.

GIBIAN, Tomas G. Sgt (CZ)/RAF
7-44/5-45   RAF No.654760
        RAF No.189762
Czech who emigrated to Canada before the war and one a the few who enlisted in this Country. Posted from No.310 (Czech) Sqn, in which in flew between May and July 1944. Posted to CIG in May 1945.
F/Sgt : 7-44, P/O : 12-44

GILLAM, Denys E.* F/L RAF
9-40/12-40   RAF No.37167
Pre-war RAF pilot posted from No.616 Sqn he was serving since September 1939. Posted in on 06.09.40 to lead B Flight from C.A.T. Jones on 06.09.40. Posted to No.306 (Polish) Sqn as CO on 01.12.40 being replaced by A.A. Dawbarn. Remained with No.306 Sqn until the end of his tour in March 1941. Second tour of operations as CO No.615 Sqn between July 1941 - February 1942. CO Duxford Wing, the first Typhoon Wing between March and October 1942. CO No.146 Wing in December 1943 - January 1944 and between July 1944 and February 1945. Eight confirmed victories, one being shared, with No.616, 312 Sqns, Dunkirk, Battle

D.E. GILLAM

of Britain, 1940, Europe, 1941. DSO [No.615 Sqn], BAR and 2ⁿᵈ BAR [No.146 Wing], DFC [No.616 Sqn], BAR [No.615 Sqn]. AFC [09.06.38].

GUNDRY, Kenneth C. P/O RAF
12-40/1-41   RAF No.81371
Posted from No.257 Sqn in which he was serving since August. Posted to No.145 Sqn, later serving with No.112 Sqn from April 1942 onwards.
†22.05.42, Kittyhawk I AK787, No.112 Sqn, Lybia.

HANZLICEK, Otto Sgt (CZ)/RAF
9-404/10-40 (†)   RAF No.787697
Pre-war CzAF pilot, serving with Air Regiment 3. In June 1939 he escaped to France via Poland joining the *Armée de l' Air* on arrival. On 01.12.39 posted to GC II/5. On 11.05.40 with two other pilots he claimed the destruction of a He111 followed by another shared Bf109 on 18.05.40 but was shot down himself. After the fall France he escaped to United Kingdom via North Africa and Gibraltar, arriving in August. Killed during a training flight when he had to bail out but drowned in the mud of the estuary of the Mersey River.

HARTMAN, Jiri P/O (CZ)/RAF
8-41/10-41   RAF No.81907
Pre-war CzAF pilot serving with Air Regiment 1. Escaped to France via Poland, joined the *Armée de l'*

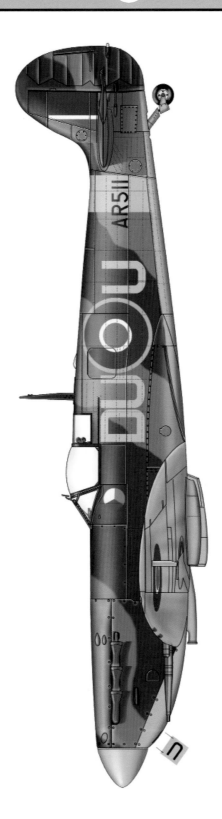

Supermarine Spitfire Mk.VC AR511, No.312 (Czechoslovak) Squadron, Flight Sergeant R. Ossendorf, Harrowbeer, September 1942.

J. HLADO

HLADO, Jaroslav**   S/L   (cz)/RAF
4-44/11-44   RAF No.125414
Posted from No.11 Group. Pre-war CzAF observation and fighter pilot with Air Regiment 1 & 4. Former member of Czechoslovak competition team before the war at Zurich, Switzerland, 1937, then test pilot of Avia aircraft factory. Escaped to Ukraine (Soviet Union) in August 1940, but was put into jail until July 1941 and was released to Czechoslovak Military Group hands in Moscow. Sent to the UK where he arrived in May 1942 and sent to No.61 OTU for refreshing training. Posted to No.131 Sqn (January 1943 - February 1943), and No.222 Sqn between May and November 1943. Posted to No.312 Sqn for his second tour of operations in April 1944, becoming the CO two weeks later. Posted to Czechoslavak Wing in November as CO, remaining at this posting until August 1945. DSO [No.134 Wing].

DFC : 31.10.44

HLOBIL, Alois*   P/O   (cz)/RAF
9-40/11-40   RAF No.82547
Pre-war CzAF pilot, with Air Regiment 4. In July 1939 he escaped to France via Poland. Joined the *Armée de l' Air*. After re-training posted to GC II/4 in January 1940, flying Curtisses. Shared a Hs126 on 05.06.40. After the Armistice he escaped to North Africa and then sailed to the United Kingdom. He enlisted to the RAF and on 05.09.40, he was posted to No.312 Sqn as Czechoslovak leader of B flight for one day only pending D.E. Gillam's arrival. In November he was withdrawn from operational duty due to his age, 34, and served as a test pilot at No.8 MU. In August 1941 he was transferred to Czechoslovak Air Ministry in London. No more operational postings until the end of war.
F/L : 6-41

Air but saw no action. In June 1940 he arrived to England and on 6th August was posted to No.310 (Czech) Sqn. In September, he was posted to No.12 OTU for retraining. Then served with No.4 FPP and No.8 MU till June 1941 when he was posted to No.55 OTU then to No.312 (Czech) Sqn in August. Posted to No.607 Sqn four months later, but after nine days he was posted to No.111 Sqn until June 1942 and return to No.310 Sqn. Completed his tour in June 1943. Second tour of operations with No.310 Sqn once again. Last Squadron's CO from 15.09.44 onwards. After the war he served with the new CzAF, being CO of fighter regiment 10 & 8. After Communist coup he escaped to Great Britain and again joined the RAF. He served with Nos.247, 288 and 275 Sqns respectively. DFC [No.310 (Czech) Sqn].

HAVLICEK, Miroslav   W/O   (cz)/RAF
5-45/8-45 @   RAF No.788161
Posted from No.53 OTU. A late arrival, after VE-Day. Completed a previous tour with No.313 (Czech) Sqn between December 1942 and June 1944.

HEKL, Frantisek   F/O   (cz)/RAF
8-41/10-41 (†)   RAF No.87619
Posted from No.52 OTU. During a training flight hit water of Lake Loch Doon and was killed.

HOLECEK, Rudolf   P/O   (cz)/RAF
9-40/9-40   RAF No.81890
Pre-war CzAF fighter pilot in Air Regiment 4. With *Armée de l'Air* 1939-1940 serving with GC I/8 flying Blochs then arrived to England in June 1940. Founder member of No.310 Sqn in July 1940. In September posted to No.312 (Czech) Sqn just for a week, before returning to No.310 (Czech) Sqn until the end of his tour in July 1941. Between July 1941 and March 1942 he served at Flying Control Officer with No.313 (Czech) Sqn. No more operational postings until the end of war, being

H. HRBACEK

posted to CIG from June 1942 and the end of war. Remained with the new CzAF after 1945 but left his country after the Communist coup in 1948.

HOLZNER, Bedrich Sgt (CZ)/RAF
7-44/8-45 @ RAF No.788097
Posted from Czech Depot. Former ground crew (armourer) with the Squadron before to be accepted for a pilot course.
F/Sgt : 10-44, W/O : 3-45, P/O : 6-45

HRBACEK, Hugo* S/L (CZ)/RAF
4-45/5-45 RAF No.87618
Posted from CIG. Czech born in Italy. Pre-war CzAF fighter pilot with Air Regiment 4, escaping to France in May 1939. With GC I/7 flying Moranes based in Lebannon between January and June 1940 before escaping to the UK in October 1940. First tour of operations with No.310 (Czech) Sqn between May 1942 and October 1943. Returned to the same unit in January 1944 as CO for his second tour. On 21.05.44 shot down by *flak* near Lisieux (France) while attacking a train. Crash landed, evaded capture with the

help of the French Resistance returning to the UK on 19.08.44. Then served at CIG before being posted as CO No.312 Sqn in April 1945. Remained with the new CzAF after 1945, became CO of Air Regiment 7 at Brno. In 1946 CO of Air Regiment 5. He left his country shortly after the Communist coup in 1948 and rejoined the RAF.

HRUSKA, Karel Sgt (CZ)/RAF
6-44/8-45 @ RAF No.787837
Former ground staff with the Squadron as a wireless mechanic, before being accepted for a pilot course.
F/Sgt : 9-44

IEVERS, Norman L. F/L (IRE)/RAF
10-40/12-40 RAF No.37812
Irish in SSC since 1936. During the first months of war, served as flying instructor. Posted in to gain combat experience. Posted to A&AEE until July 1941 when he was posted to No.257 Sqn until September when he was posted to No.19 Sqn. In November he was posted to Middle East and became CO No.80 Sqn between November 1941 and February 1942. Later served in Far East at non-operational postings. Released from the RAF in 1944 as a Squadron Leader.

JANEBA, Josef Sgt (CZ)/RAF
9-40/10-41, 3-42/5-42 (†) RAF No.787707
  RAF No.113884
Pre-war CzAF pilot, serving with Air Regiment 1. In June 1939 he escaped to France, joining the *Armée de l' Air* and after retraining was posted to GC II/5 on 01.12.39. On 02.03.40 he became the first Czechoslovakian pilot to claim a victory of WW2 sharing it with two French pilots (a Do17P probably destroyed). On 11.05.40 he shot down another bomber, this time He111, shared with two other pilots including the Czech Hanzlicek. Shot down on 06.06.40 but evaded capture. After the fall of France he escaped to England via North Africa and Gibraltar and in August he enlisted in the RAF. Posted to No.312 Sqn, becoming a founder member of the Squadron. Posted out at the end of his first tour in October 1941. He was commissioned and in March 1942 he returned to No.312 Sqn for his second tour of operations. Shortly after take-off on 02.05.42, his wingman'aircraft Sgt Vaculik cut off the tail of his own Spitfire. He bailed out too low and his chute failed to open and he was killed.

J. JANEBA

JASKE, Josef * P/O (CZ)/RAF
9-40/7-41 RAF No.83226
Pre-war CzAF pilot with Air Regiment 4. In June 1939 he escaped to Poland and subsequently to France. Enlisted in the *Armée de l' Air* and posted to GC II/5 in December 1939. Shared a probably destroyed Do17 on 23.04.40. On 16.05.40 he destroyed a He111 south of Sedan but was himself shot down. With his unit he retreated to North Africa and subsequently he went to the United Kingdom, becoming later a founder member of the Squadron. On 28.05.41 he was promoted and became leader of A flight, when C.A. Cooke left. Posted to No.313 (Czech) Sqn as CO on 20.07.41 being replaced by J. Cermak. Remained with No.313 Sqn until the end of his tour in December 1941. Served at Czechoslovak Air Ministry as liaison officer at No.10 Group. On 26.11.42 he was flying the aicraft in which Group Captain E. Cizek was killed (see above), suffering himself only injuries. Subsequently, he became Assistant of the Czechoslovak Military and Air Attaché in Canada. After Communist coup in February 1948 he was turned out from the Air Force. He escaped and again joined the RAF.
F/O : 1-41, F/L : 6-41

JONES, Cyril A.T.* F/L RAF
8-40/9-40 RAF No.43693
Posted from No.611 Sqn, he served with since April 1940. Posted in on 29.08.40 to lead the B flight but

one week after his arrival posted to No.616 Sqn. Replaced by D.E. Gillam on the 6th September. Badly wounded in action on 05.11.40 and withdrawn from operations. Later CO No.79 sqn in India between February 1942 and February 1944. **DFC** [No.79 Sqn].

KARASEK, Zikmund Sgt (CZ)/RAF
10-40/7-41, 3-42/6-42 RAF No.787621
Pre-war CzAF cadet with Air Regiment 1. On 27.04.39, he escaped to France via Poland. Joined the *Armée de l' Air* and in May 1940 but never flew in operations. Escaped to England on 19.06.40. After completing his training was posted to No.312 Sqn. Posted to No.1 Sqn in April 1941 and later in September, to No.258 Sqn. Remaining one month with this unit, he was posted to No.54 Sqn, and to No.65 Sqn in November 1941 completed his tour in December. Returned to the Squadron for his second tour in March 1942 as Flight Sergeant. In June 1942, due of health troubles, he was not authorized to fly again. Ground duties until demobilizaton in November 1945.

KASAL, Karel * F/L (CZ)/RAF
6-42/11-42, 1-43/6-44 RAF No.81893
Posted from No.313 (Czech) Sqn. Known as "*Pablo*". Pre-war CzAF pilot with Air Regiment 6. In 1939 he escaped to France. Enlisted in the *Armée de l' Air* but saw no action. Arrived in England on 17.06.40. After

retraining he was posted to No.607 Sqn in November 1940 remaining with until May 1941 when he was posted to No.313 (Czech) Sqn as founder member. On 19.06.42 he became the leader of B Flight from T. Vybiral. Wounded in action, he was replaced by A. Vrana on 25.08.42 until 19.09.42, but left the B flight on 15.11.42 relinquished command to T. Vybiral. Second tour of operations with the Squadron again beeween January 1943 and June 1944, becomping A flight leader from 01.02.43 until the end of his tour when he was posted to No.19 Sector. He was replacing V. Kaslik, and was replaced by J. Keprt. Posted out, tour expired. In September 1944, he was posted to No.313 (Czech) Sqn as CO until November 1944. Returned to the Squadron in June 1945.

KASLIK, Viktor*   F/O   (CZ)/RAF
8-41/2-43, 5-43/7-43   RAF No.83227
Pre-war CzAF pilot with Air Regiment 4. In May 1939 he escaped to France via Poland to enlist in the *Armée de l' Air*. He was posted to GC I/9 in Tunisia where he flew MS.406s. After the fall of France he escaped to the United Kingdom. Joined the RAF and in December 1940 he was serving at non-operational units before to be posted in. On 30.05.42 he became the A flight leader succeeding J. Cermak. At the end of his tour, on 01.02.43, he was replaced by K. Kasal. Served at No.2 DF. Returned to the Squadron as B flight leader between 01.06.43 and 01.07.43, replacing T. Vybiral. Posted out to become a liaison officer at No.10 Group of Fighter Command. He was replaced by V. Slouf. In February 1944 he became the liaison officer of Czechoslovak wing at No.84 Group of 2nd TAF.
F/L : 12-41

KEPRT, Josef*   Sgt   (CZ)/RAF
9-40/3-41, 5-42/8-43, 3-44/10-44   RAF No.787695
   RAF No.86138
See biography. A Flight leader between 10.06.44 and 01.10.44, succeeding K. Kasal. He was replaced by V. Slouf.
F/L : 5-43
DFC : 14.02.45

KIMLICKA, Bohuslav   P/O   (CZ)/RAF
9-40/10-40   RAF No.82553
Posted from No.310 (Czech) Sqn. Pre-war CzAF pilot with Air Regiment 6 and 2, escaping to France in 1939. Joined the *Armée de l' Air* and served with GC

II/10 and GC I/6 in May and June 1940. After the fall of France he fled to the UK via North Africa and Gibraltar. Posted to No.310 (Czech) Sqn as founder member, but returned to his former unit one week later. With No.313 (Czech) Sqn between September 1942 and January 1943. Second tour of operations with No.310 Sqn between June 1943 and January 1944. Then he served at personal department of Czechoslovak Air Ministry in London.

KLAN, Jan*   P/O   (CZ)/RAF
9-40/6-41   RAF No.83228
Pre-war CzAF pilot with Air Regiment 2 and 4 in 1938, then Czech Police Air Patrol in 1938 - 1939. On 26.05.39, escaped to France via Poland. Later joined the *Armée de l' Air*, and after retraining he was posted to GC II/5 on 01.12.39. Claimed his first victory, a Bf109 on 23.04.40. In May - June 1940 claimed a destroyed Bf109 and a shared destroyed Hs126, Do17 & He111, and three probables. After the Armistice he escaped to the United Kingdom. On 17.11.40 became A Flight leader after J. Duda, relinquished command to C.A. Cooke on 17.12.40 and in May 1941 became the CO of the Squadron. But due to bad health conditions, he was withdrawn from operational duty and posted to

J.KLAN

Josef KEPRT
RAF No.787695 (NCO)
RAF No.86138 (Officer)

Josef Keprt was born on 28th June, 1910. He enlisted in the Czechoslovakian Air Force in 1928 and graduated two years later. In 1934 he completed training as a fighter pilot and joined 36.*stihaci letka* (Fighter Flight 36) of Air Regiment 2. On 14th June 1939, following the German occupation of his country, he escaped to France, by way of Poland. He enlisted in the Foreign Legion but when war broke out in 1939 he was posted to CIC (Fighter OTU) at Chartres. On graduation he was posted, as a Sergeant, to GC III/3 at Toul-Ochey on 1st December, 1939. This unit was equipped with MS406s and on 21st December he took part in the first air combat involving Czechoslovak pilots serving with the *Armée de l' Air*, and the Luftwaffe. The German "Blitzkrieg" in the west began on 10th May, 1940 and three days later Josef Keprt gained his first victory when, over Namur, he shared a probable Hs126 and the following day a Do17P. Late in May his squadron was re-equipped with Dewoitine D.520s and on 16th June the unit claimed its last victories when Josef Keprt, and six other pilots, claimed a Hs126 (actually a Fi156 of VIII *Flieger Korps*). Following the fall of France he reached the United Kingdom and enlisted in the RAF and, after being trained in British procedures, he joined No.312 (Czechoslovak) Squadron on 5th September 1940, once again with the rank of Sergeant. During a training flight on 10th September the engine of his Hurricane caught fire however he managed to bale out and his aircraft crashed south of Cambridge. This was the Squadron's first accident. Over the next few days the Squadron was initiated into the Battle of Britain.

On 24th March, 1941 he was posted to No.96 Squadron where he flew Defiants at night and was commissioned in May 1941. Returning to base from a sortie on 2nd August 1941 the engine of his Defiant failed and he broke his left arm when he crash-landed at Cranage airfield, and had to be taken to hospital. The damage was extensive and it was not until 3rd May, 1942 that he returned to No.312 Squadron and was promoted to the rank of Flying Officer. On 19th August he was engaged in combat over Dieppe during Operation *Jubilee* and on this day he flew two sorties damaging a FW190, and destroying a Do217. He completed his second tour of operations on 10th August, 1943 and did not return to the Squadron for another seven months. On 10th June, 1944, shortly after the invasion of France, he was appointed to lead A Flight and on 2nd October, he was posted to Inspectorat of Czechoslovak Air Ministry as a liaison officer at Air Defence Command. For his military service he was awarded the Czechoslovak War Cross (four times), the French *Croix de Guerre* and the DFC, the latter on 14th February, 1945. He returned to Czechoslovakia on 19th August, 1945 however after the Communist coup he was persecuted. Josef Keprt died in Brno on 29th July, 1976.

Czechoslovak Air Ministry, later being posted to No.11 Group of Fighter Command as a liaison officer as Wing Commander. In 1942 he asked to come back to front line as Flight Lieutenant. Being retrained at No.51 OTU he was posted to No.605 Sqn in July 1942 flying Havoc Mk.I remaining until October 1942 when he was posted to Czech flight of No.68 Sqn until June 1943. Volunteered to serve with the Czech Fighter Regiment in Soviet Union he was discharged from RAF on 01.02.44, becoming the deputy commander of this unit on 01.06.44. When was formed 1st Czechoslovak Composite Air Division he was appointed chief of staff. After the war he was the first commander of the Air Transport Group of CzAF. In 1946- 1948, became deputy of Czechoslovak Military and Air Attaché in Moscow. Being turned out from the army in May 1949 he subsequently emigrated to the USA.
F/L : 12-40, S/L : 6-41

KLOBOUCNIK, Josef   P/O   (CZ)/RAF
9-40/2-41   RAF No.83971
Pre-war CzAF Pilot with Air Regiment 4. Joined the *Armée de l'Air* in October 1939. Was trained but never flew in operations. Became founder member of the Squadron. Posted to No.96 Sqn, a night fighter Sqn until July 1941, when he was posted to No.68 Sqn.
F/O : 1-41
†22.10.41, Beaufighter IF R2099, No.68 Sqn, United Kingdom.

KOCFELDA, Pavel   F/Sgt   (CZ)/RAF
4-43/2-44   RAF No.787471
                                          RAF No.149254
Posted from No.57 OTU. Pre-war CzAF Pilot. After retraining, posted to No.313 (Czech) Sqn (January 1942 - April 1943). Discharged from RAF on 01.02.44 to serve with the 1st Czechoslovak Fighter Air Regiment, claiming two victories over Slovakia, one being shared. After re-organization of CzAF on the Eastern Front he was transferred to 2nd Czechoslovak Fighter Air Regiment. After the war he remained in the duty till retirement in the 70s.
P/O : 7-43

KOHOUT, Josef   Sgt   (CZ)/RAF
6-42/5-43, 11-43/1-45   RAF No.787389
                                          RAF No.177438
Posted from No.313 (Czech) Sqn. Pre-war CzAF cadet under training. On 25.05.39 he escaped to

P.KOCFELDA

France via Poland. He joined the *Armée de l' Air* but saw no action in May-June 1940 his training being not completed yet. On 18.06.40 he sailed to the United Kingdom. Completing his training he was posted to No.601 Sqn until March 1942. Subsequently served with No.610 Sqn (March - May 1942) and No.313 (Czech) Sqn (May - June 1942). Posted out at the end of his tour in May 1943. After the war he served at Czechoslovak Air Force but emigrated after Communist coup.
F/Sgt : 10-42, W/O : 1-44, P/O : 1-45

KONVICKA, Jindrich   Sgt   (CZ)/RAF
5-44/12-44   RAF No.788221
Posted from No.313 (Czech) Sqn, he was serving with February. Posted to Czech Depot, tour expired.
F/Sgt : 8-44, W/O : 11-44

KOPECKY, Zdenek   Sgt   (CZ)/RAF
12-44/8-45 @   RAF No.787474
Posted from No.57 OTU. Formerly with No.11 Czech Infantry Battalion in the Middle East and North Africa. In January 1943 he arrived to the United Kingdom and enlisted in the RAF.
F/Sgt : 1-45

KOPECEK, Vladimir Sgt (CZ)/RAF
6-42/4-43, 6-43/11-44 RAF No.787483
RAF No.158013

Posted from No.65 Sqn. Pre-war CzAF pilot with Air Regiment 5. Escaped to France via Poland on 17.04.39. If he joined the *Armée de l'Air* in 1939, he never saw action and escaped to England. After his training he was posted to No.65 Sqn in September 1941 until being posted in until the end of his tour in April 1943. Posted to No.1 ADF at that time. Another tour with No.312 Sqn between June 1943 (posted from No.57 OTU) and November 1944 when he was posted to Czech Depot. No more operational postings until the end of war. He returned to Czechoslovakia but after Communist coup he emigrated to the United Kingdom and enlisted again in the RAF as flying instructor at Ahlhom in Germany. Killed in flying accident on 17.11.55 during a training flight on Meteor T.7, falling into unconsciousness. His pupil managed to land but he died due of overpressure.
F/Sgt : 10-42, P/O : 9-43, F/O : 3-44

KOSINA, Karel Sgt (CZ)/RAF
9-40/9-40 RAF No.787539
Posted from No.310 (Czech) Sqn. Pre-war CzAF Pilot escaping to France via Poland in 1939. With the

F.KOTIBA

Armée de l'Air serving with GC III/7 in March 1940. On 17.06.40 he was posted to Czechoslovak flight of GC I/6. After the Armistice he escaped to the United Kingdom. Posted to No.310 (Czech) Sqn in August 1940 remaining six weeks with this unit but returned to No.310 Sqn one week later until December 1940 when he was posted to No.19 Sqn remaining with it until the end of his tour in August 1941. Returned briefly with No.310 Sqn in March - April 1942. Two more tours of operations with No.310 Sqn until the end of war, December 1942 - May 1944 and November 1944 - May 1945.

KOTIBA, Frantisek F/Sgt (CZ)/RAF
12-42/6-43 RAF No.787385
Pre-war CzAF Pilot. With the *Armée de l'Air* in December 1939 but saw no action. In 1940 he joined the RAF and after retraining on British planes he became flying instructor in No.3 EFTS. In January 1942 he was posted to No.124 Sqn before being posted to No.313 (Czech) Sqn until May 1942. Returned to operation in December 1942 with No.312 Sqn. Posted to No.66 Sqn in June 1943 until August 1943. Twin-engined pilot course in 1944 and was killed during a training flight.
†19.06.44, Beaufighter IF X7705, No.51 OTU, United Kingdom.

KOUKAL, Josef P/O (CZ)/RAF
5-43/8-43 RAF No.120764
Pre-war CzAF pilot with Air Regiment 1. In the late 30s he was also a test pilot at Benes - Mraz Company. Escaped from his country on 12.08.39 and served with the Polish Air Force and eventually was captured by the Soviets. He escaped from captivity and reached France via Romania and Middle East. Arrived in England in July 1940, being posted at once to No.310 (Czech) Sqn as founder member. Severely wounded in action on 07.09.40 and taken to hospital with various bad burns. After recovery he was posted to No.312 Sqn. Posted to No.1 ADF on 01.08.43 serving with delivery units and CIG until the end of war. One confirmed victory with No.310 Sqn, Battle of Britain, 1940.

KOWAC, Vladimir W/O (CZ)/RAF
1-45/8-45 @ RAF No.787274
Posted from No.57 OTU. Escaped to France when the Country was occupied. He joined the *Armée de l'Air*, but saw no action and escaped to England. Completed

one operational tour with No.311 (Czech) Sqn as Air Gunner in 1941 - 1942. Later accepted for a pilot course and posted in on completion of his training.

KRUML, Tomas P/O (CZ)/RAF
9-40/2-42 RAF No.83229

Pre-war CzAF pilot with Air Regiment 1 and later at Military Technical & Aeronautical Institute. On 15.05.39 he escaped to France via Poland. Joined the *Armée de l' Air* and on 17.05.40 he was posted to GC III/3. One shared confirmed victory with the French. After the fall of France he escaped to North Africa. Subsequently he reached the United Kingdom via Gibraltar and joined the RAF in August and on the following month became a founder member of the Squadron. Posted to No.53 OTU in February 1942, tour expired. Another tour in October 1942 with No.66 Sqn until January 1943, then to No.131 Sqn until February and No.122 Sqn until the end of his tour in August 1943. Subsenquently he was posted to Czechoslovak Air Ministry and later to Fighter Command. In June 1944 he was posted to the Air Ministry, where he led a Czechoslovak group in charge of study training methods. In 1945 he served at several headquarters and in May he was posted to Central Fighter Establishment in Tangmere. He became the first Czechoslovak pilot who flew on jet airplane, flying a Meteor. He served with CzAF with the rank *plukovnik* (Colonel) till his retirement in October 1967, nearly twenty years without promotion. He was one of few formely RAF pilots who served till retirement.
F/O : 1-41, F/L : 12-41

KRUTA, Frantisek Sgt (CZ)/RAF
10-40/7-41, 8-43/2-44 RAF No.787674
RAF No.158014

Pre-war CzAF pilot with Air Regiment 4, escaping to France via Poland on 15.04.39. With the *Armée de l'Air* in 1939 - 1940 but saw no action reaching England on 17.06.40. After a short retraining posted in. Posted to No.245 Sqn in July 1941 and in November to No.32 Sqn. In July 1942, posted to No.313 (Czech) Sqn, completing his tour with it in December 1942. Returned to No.313 Sqn for another tour in June 1943 until August when he was posted again to No.312 Sqn as Warrant Officer. Volunteered to serve in Soviet Union, he was discharged from RAF on 01.02.44. As a member of 1st Czechoslovak Fighter Air Regiment he took part to the combats over Slovakia during September 1944. Shot down by *flak*, on 19.09.44, he became a prisoner of war. After the war he was demobilized and in 1948 he emigrated to the United Kingdom and later to Australia.
P/O : 8-43

F.KRUTA

KUBAK, Josef Sgt (CZ)/RAF
9-40/3-41 RAF No.787983

Posted from No.310 (Czech) Sqn. Pre-war CzAF pilot. After the occupation of his country he escaped to France via Poland. Enlisted in the *Armée de l' Air* but saw no operational flying. After the fall of France he went to the United Kingdom. First posting at No.310 Sqn. Posted to No.312 Sqn for nine days only returning to No.310 Sqn. Served later with No.19 Sqn in March 1941, No.118 Sqn in April 1941 and No.32 Sqn (April - May 1941). Withdrawn from operational duty on 30.04.41, becoming a flying instructor until the War's end.

KUCERA, Jaroslav Sgt (CZ)/RAF
9-41/12-41 (†) RAF No.787665

Posted from No.605 Sqn. Escaped to France via Poland in 1939. He joined the *Armée de l' Air* and after retraining he was posted to GCD I/55 on 19.05.40. After the Armistice he escaped to Great Britain. After retraining, posted to No.245 Sqn in

October 1940 and to No.605 Sqn in December that year remaining with it until September 1941. Killed during a mock fight over Ayshire.

KUCERA, Otmar Sgt (CZ)/RAF
4-41/4-42 RAF No.787658
RAF No.112548

Posted from No.111 Sqn. Pre-war CzAF pilot with Air Regiment 2. Escaped to France at his second attempt in December 1939 arriving in March 1940 enlisting in the *Armée de l'Air*. Arrived too late to see any action during the Battle of France, but managed to escape to the United Kingdom. After being retrained, he was posted to No.111 Sqn (October 1940 - April 1941). Posted to No.313 (Czech) Sqn until June 1942. Another tour with No.313 Sqn between January 1943 and May 1944, returning as CO to the same unit in November that year for his last tour. He remained with the new CzAF after the war. Trying to escape from his country after the Communist coup, he was arrested and put into jail. Soon released by lack of evidence for conspiracy, he left the Air Force working as labourer. Seven confirmed victories, two being shared with Nos.111, 312 and 313 Sqns, Europe, 1941 -1943. DFC [No.313 (Czech) Sqn].
P/O : 11-41

KUKUCKA, Josef Sgt (CZ)/RAF
5-44/3-45 RAF No.654729
RAF No.95063

Slovak. Posted from No.313 (Czech) Sqn he served

O. KUCERA

three weeks only. Canadian citizen. Enlisted in Canada, being a son of Slovakian emigrants in this Country. Posted out, tour expired. Later commissioned.
F/Sgt : 9-44, W/O : 11-44, P/O : 6-45

LAMBERTON, Karel Sgt (CZ)/RAF
10-44/8-45 @ RAF No.788101

Posted from No.310 (Czech) he was serving with since July 1944. Former ground staff member with No.312 Sqn in July 1941 later accepted for a pilot course. After the completion of his training was posted to No.310 (Czech) Sqn.
F/Sgt : 3-45, P/O : 6-45

LASKA, Jan P/O (CZ)/RAF
10-40/9-41 RAF No.82558

Pre-war CzAF Pilot. Enlisted in the *Armée de l'Air* in October 1939 but saw no action. In late summer 1940 he joined the RAF and posted in. Posted to No.245 Sqn and to No.32 Sqn in September the same year, remaining with the latter until to be posted to No.313 (Czech) Sqn in July 1942. Tour completed in April 1943. In October 1943 he returned to No.313 Sqn for another tour. On 26.04.44 he crashed landed after a collision with another plane of his unit, dying later at the hospital.
†26.04.44, Spitfire IX MJ979, No.313 (Czech) Sqn, United Kingdom.

LISKA, Antonin F/O (CZ)/RAF
8-41/6-42 RAF No.87623

Posted from No.1 Sqn. Pre-war CzAF officer with Air Regiment 1. Escaped to Poland on 16.08.39, but after the invasion of this country, he fell into Soviet hands and put into jail. Released during Spring 1940, he reached via Roumania and Turkey the United Kingdom in October 1940. Retrained he served with to No.1 Sqn between May and August 1941. Badly injured in flying accident on 29.06.42. When he recovered, his operational career was over. He served with the new CzAF after the war. He became the commander of Air Transport Regiment. Turned out after the Communist coup.
F/L : 3-42

LISKA, Vratislav Sgt (CZ)/RAF
6-44/5-45@ RAF No.788366

Posted from No.53 OTU. Previously a wireless operator accepted for a pilot course. Later commis-

M. LISKUTIN

sioned. After the war he served with Air Regiment 25 of the new CzAF. Killed in flying accident on 11.10.48 (Mosquito FB.VI HR255).
F/Sgt : 9-44, W/O : 4-45, P/O : 6-45

LISKUTIN, Miroslav Sgt (cz)/RAF
11-41/5-43, 8-43/11-44 RAF No.787424
RAF No.158235
Posted from No.145 Sqn. Pre-war CzAF member under training as fighter pilot. In 1939 he escaped to France via Poland. When the war broke out he joined the *Armée de l' Air* but could not complete his training as fighter pilot before the fall of France. Subsequently he escaped to the United Kingdom. After the completion of his training was first posted to No.145 Sqn (September - November 1941). Tour expired in May 1943. Commissioned in July 1943 he returned to the Squadron for another tour, remaining with it until the end of his tour and posted to Czech Depot. After the war he served with Fighter Air Regiment 7 of the new CzAF. After the Communist coup he escaped to Austria in June 1948 and rejoined the RAF leaving it in August 1962. One shared confirmed victory, No.312 Sqn, Europe, 1942.
F/Sgt : 10-42, F/O : 3-44
DFC : 14.02.45

LOUCKY, Frantisek Sgt (cz)/RAF
6-42/7-42, 12-42/1-44 RAF No.787437
Posted from No.65 Sqn. As eighteen years old he was

not accepted by CzAF for military service in 1930, due of consequences of injurie he suffered when he was fourteen. Therefore, he got his civil private pilot's licence. On 17.12.39 he escaped from Czechoslovakia via Hungary, where he spent four months in prison, continuing his travel via Yugoslavia, Greece, Turkey, Lebanon and Egypt, reaching France on 15.05.40. Next month he escaped to the United Kingdom. After his training, posted to No.65 Sqn in September 1941 before being posted to No.312 Sqn in June 1942, but posted to Czechoslovak Depot the following month. Returned to the Squadron in December 1942 for another tour. Volunteered to serve in Soviet Union, he was discharged from RAF on 01.02.44. Member of 1st Czechoslovak Fighter Air Regiment in Slovakia during the National Uprising. During Spring 1945 he served with 2nd Czechoslovak Fighter Air Regiment. After the war he was demobilized.

MACENAUER, Antonin F/L (cz)/RAF
8-43/12-43 RAF No.82619
Pre-war Pilot of CzAF. In 1940 he joined the RAF. At first he served with No.311 (Czechoslovak) Sqn as a navigator till 1942. Subsenquently he was accepted for a pilot training and posted in as supernumerary Flight Lieutenant on completion of his training. Posted out in December 1943 and in early 1944 he was posted to No.291 (Army Co-operation) Sqn. In December he was serving with No.4 DF. No more details available.

MACHEK, Otokar Sgt (cz)/RAF
1-45/8-45 @ RAF No.788496
Posted from No.57 OTU. Former member of No.11 Czech Infantry Battalion in Middle East and North Africa. In January 1943 he was sent to the United Kingdom to be trained as fighter pilot.
F/Sgt : 3-45

MALY, Milan Sgt (cz)/RAF
5-45/8-45 @ RAF No.788498
Former member of No.11 Czech Infantry Battalion in Middle East and North Africa. In January 1943 he was sent to the United Kingdom to be trained as fighter pilot.

MARES, Frantisek F/Sgt (cz)/RAF
6-42/9-42, 3-43/6-43 RAF No.787653
Posted from No.313 (Czech) Sqn. Pre-war CzAF member still under training when the country was occupied. Escaped to France via Poland on 16.06.39.

© www.venturapublications.com

Supermarine Spitfire LF.IXC MJ637, No.312 (Czechoslovak) Squadron, Warrant Officer F. Vravrinek, Mendlesham, February 1944.

Joined the *Armée de l'Air* but could not complete his training. Evacuated to England on 25.06.40. Completed his training with the RAF and posted to No.601 in November 1940. Posted to No.610 Sqn in March 1942 until May when he was posted to No.313 (Czech) Sqn before being posted to No.312 Sqn the following month. Posted to No.2 DF, tour expired. Returned to the Squadron for his second tour of operations in March 1943, but was posted to No.61 OTU in June due to problems with his eyes. Back to operational units with No.310 (Czech) Sqn between July and October 1944, but had to be taken off from operations due to his continued eyes problems. Commissioned in September 1944. Settled in England after the war. Four confirmed victories, three being shared with Nos.601 and 610 Sqns, Europe, 1941 - 1942.

W/O : 10-42

DFM : 03.09.42

F.MARES

MAYER, Jan   Sgt   (CZ)/RAF

11-41/7-42, 9-42/12-42, 5-45/8-45 @   RAF No.787384

Posted from No.145 Sqn. Pre-war CzAF pilot with Air Regiment 3. On 10.08.39, he escaped to France. With Czechoslovak Army Depot in 1940. Was posted to its air group and on 06.06.40 arrived at Bordeaux. Next month he reached the United Kingdom. After the completion of his training he was posted to No.145 Sqn (September - November 1941). Following health problem, he was took off from operations for two months, being back in September. Posted to No.61 OTU as a flying instructor at the end of his tour. Returned to the Squadron shortly after VE-Day as Warrant Officer posted from No.57 OTU.

F/Sgt : 10-42

MEIER, Augustin   Sgt   (CZ)/RAF

2-43/2-43   RAF No.788332

Posted from OTU. Posted to No.310 (Czech) eight days after his arrival remaining with this unit until his death.

†21.05.44, Spitfire IX MK116, No.310 (Czech) Sqn, United Kingdom.

MENSIK, Jozef   Sgt   (CZ)/RAF

10-40/7-41   RAF No.787663

Slovak. Posted from No.6 OTU. Pre-war CzAF with Air Regiment 2. Escaped to France on 01.12.39 and in April 1940 he arrived at Czechoslovak Depot in Agde (South of France) but saw no action. After the fall of France he was evacuated to the United Kingdom. Shot down on 08.07.41 over France, he evaded capture but was put into jail in Spain before reaching Gibraltar in October and on 21.10.41 he arrived in England. He was commissioned and in September 1942 went at No.54 OTU for twin-engined course to become a night fighter. In December 1942, posted to the Czech flight of No.68 Sqn until his death.

†22.04.43, Beaufighter VI V8567, No.68 Sqn, United Kingdom.

MIKULECKY, Jiri   F/O   (CZ)/RAF

7-44/8-45 @   RAF No.125413

Posted from No.1 TEU. He escaped to Poland on 25.08.39 but was captured by the Soviets and spent two years in force labour camp before to be released. In March 1942 he was one of eight Czechoslovak pilots who were sent to the United Kingdom. Sailed from Murmansk on board of HMS *Edinburg*. On 30.04.42 the cruiser was sunk but he survived. The following month he was again at sea, this time on board of HMS *Trinidad* which was also sunk. He was again rescued by a destroyed and ferried to Iceland. He subsequently reached the United Kingdom. He enlisted in the RAF and after retraining posted to No.312 Sqn. After the war, became CO of Air Regiment 4. In 1948, he escaped to Germany with V. Kopecek, V. Soukup, J. Sodek and J. Ruprecht with a Siebel 204. Joined the RAF again, serving between 1948 and 1958.

F/L : 7-44

J. MENSIK

MLEJNECKY, Frantisek W/O (CZ)/RAF
8-43/10-44 RAF No.793503
RAF No.160980

Posted from No.313 (Czech) Sqn. Pre-war CzAF pilot with Air Regiment 1. After the occupation of his country he escaped to France via Poland joining the *Armée de l' Air*. After retraining, he was posted on 20.05.40 to ELD Chartres, a week later he was transferred to GC II/10 and on 06.06.40 to GC I/6. After the fall of France he went to England. Being retrained, he was posted to No.85 Sqn, one week later to No.310

F. MLEJNECKY

(Czech) Sqn. Briefly served with No.257 Sqn in May 1941 before returning to No.310 Sqn completing his tour in January 1943. Second tour of operations starting with No.313 (Czech) Sqn in July 1943. Later commisssioned. Posted to No.1 ADF, tour expired.
P/O : 10-43, F/O : 4-44

MOTYCKA, Tomas Sgt (CZ)/RAF
11-41/3-43, 9-43/2-44 RAF No.788026
RAF No.156826

Pre-war CzAF pilot with Air Regiment 4. Escaped to Poland on 12.06.39. Joined the Polish Air Force eventually being captured by the Soviets. Released, he reached England in October 1940. One tour with the Squadron between November 1941 and March 1943, then posted in again for another tour six months later. He was commissioned and volunteered to served on the Eastern Front and discharged from RAF on 01.02.44. Became member of 1st Czechoslovak Fighter Air Regiment. He took part in the combats over Slovakia in September and October 1944.
F/Sgt : 4-42, W/O : 10-42, P/O : 7-43
†15.10.44, La-5FN No.20, 1ˢᵗ Cz Fighter Regiment, Slovakia.

MRAZ, Bohuslav Sgt (CZ)/RAF
5-43/2-44 RAF No.787603

Posted from No.57 OTU. Previously with No.313 (Czech) for a week only. Volunteered to serve in Soviet Union, was discharged from RAF on 01.02.44. After the re-training on fighters La-5FN he took part in the combats over Slovakia.
†07.10.44, La-5FN No.74, 1ˢᵗ Cz Fighter Regiment, Slovakia.

NAVRATIL, Antonin P/O (CZ)/RAF
8-40/3-41 RAF No.81897

Posted from No.310 (Czech) where he was a founder member. Pre-war CzAF pilot with Air Regiment 3. After the occupation of Czechoslovakia he escaped to France via Poland. Enlisted in the *Armée de l' Air* and on 27.12.39 was posted to GC I/8 flying Blochs. After the fall of France he flew to the United Kingdom on 17.06.40. Then various staff postings at Czechoslovak Inspectorate General (CIG) till October 1944 when he moved to Soviet Union where he finished the war as a chief of staff of the 3ʳᵈ Czech ground-attack Air Regiment.
F/O : 1-41

NOSEK, Vilem   Sgt   (CZ)/RAF

5-44/6-44 (†)   RAF No.787647

In 1939 he escaped from Czechoslovakia. He served with the *Armée de l' Air* as a ground mechanic with GC II/5. After the fall of France he escaped to the United Kingdom. At first he served as a ground mechanic with No.312 Sqn before being accepted for a pilot course. Killed on return from a combat patrol over Normandy crashing into the hill at Barnes Farm near Washington, Sussex, due of the bad weather.

NOVAK, Jaroslav   F/Sgt   (CZ)/RAF

7-41/7-42, 10-42/5-43 (†)   RAF No.787704

                                RAF No.117370

Pre-war member of the CzAF since 1933. In summer 1939 he escaped to France via Poland. When the war broke out he enlisted in the *Armée de l' Air*. In May - June 1940, he served with GC I/9. After the Armistice he escaped to the United Kingdom. Retrained and posted to No.1 Sqn until July 1941. Posted out in July 1942, tour expired. Commissioned, he returned to the Squadron for his second tour of operations in October 1942. Two confirmed victories, one being shared with No.1 Sqn, 1941. Shot down by *flak* during *Roadstead* 2 whilst attacking the target, St-Peter Port Harbour (Guernsey).

NOVOTNY, Josef   Sgt   (CZ)/RAF

8-41/4-43, 6-43/7-44, 2-45/8-45 @   RAF No.787655

                                RAF No.160797

Posted from No.1 Sqn. Reached Great Britain in 1940 and joined the RAF. First posting No.1 Sqn in April 1941. Posted to No.1 ADF in April 1943. Returned to the Squadron in June 1943 posted from No.57 OTU. Three tours of operations with No.312 Sqn. Commissioned in May 1943. Posted to Czech Depot in February 1945.

F/Sgt : 10-42, W/O : 1-43, P/O : 10-43, F/O : 4-44

OCELKA, Antonin   Sgt   (CZ)/RAF

5-43/9-44   RAF No.787772

Posted from No.57 OTU. Was not a pre-war CzAF member. Escaped from his country on 26.06.39. Reached France via Poland and enlisted in the Foreign Legion but when the war broke out he was transferred to the Czechoslovak Army in France, serving with the 1ˢᵗ Regiment as artilleryman in May - June 1940. Arrived in England on 07.07.40, enlisting to the RAF in September. Trained at No.6 School of Technical Training and in April 1941 he was posted to

No.311 (Czech) Sqn as a fitter. Accepted for a pilot course and posted to No.312 Sqn at the end of his training. Subsequently, he was posted to No.57 OTU on 4ᵗʰ May he was transferred to No.312 Sqn. Shot down by *flak* on 18.09.44 and crash-landed, becoming a PoW until the end of war. After the war he served at Czechoslovak Air Force but was killed in the accident on 01.07.49 flying a Siebel 204.

F/Sgt : 3-44

OSSENDORF, Robert   Sgt   (CZ)/RAF

1-42/6-43, 2-44/5-44, 12-44/8-45 @   RAF No.787870

                                RAF No.189192

Posted from No.57 OTU. Pupil pilot in France, still under training when France collapsed and evacuated to the UK. Completed his tour with the Squadron. Returned to the Squadron for another tour in February 1944, posted from RAF Croydon. Shot down by *flak* on 21.05.44 but managed to evade capture helped by the French Resistance returning to England on 29.07.44. No.288 Sqn between in October and November 1944, then No.287 Sqn until December and reposted to No.312 Sqn as Pilot Officer.

F/Sgt : 10-42, W/O : 3-44, F/O : 7-45

PERINA, Frantisek   P/O   (CZ)/RAF

9-40/12-42   RAF No.83241

Pre-war CzAF pilot with Air Regiment 2. Member of the

R. OSSENDORF

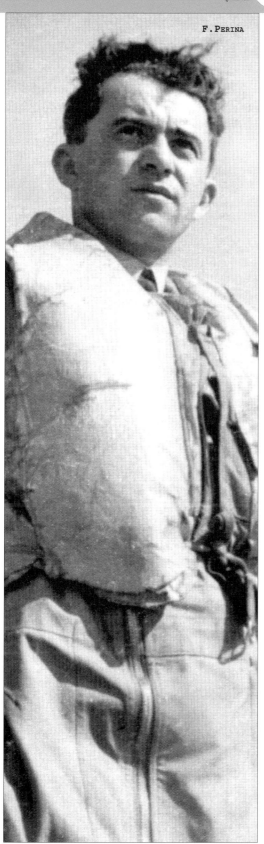

F. PERINA

Czechoslovakian team of the International Air Competition in Zürich in 1937 where he met the French *capitaine* J.M. Accart he will fight with three years later. Escaped from his country on 26.06.39 via Poland. Reaching France a couple of weeks later, he was retrained and posted to GC I/5 commanded by J.M. Accart. Evacuated to North Africa, he escaped to Gibraltar in July 1940. Founder member of the Squadron, remaining with it until the end of his tour in December 1942. No more operational postings until the end of war serving at various staff postings. Remained wih the new CzAF after the war but escaped again from his country after the Communist coup and joined again the RAF (1949 - 1954). Emigrated to Canada and later to the USA. He returned to the Czech Republic in 1993. Twelve confirmed victories, nine being shared, with the French, 1940, and No.312 Sqn, 1942.
F/O : 2-42, F/L : 9-42

PERINA, Karel   F/Sgt   (CZ)/RAF
5-44/2-45   RAF No.788140
Posted from No.313 (Czech) Sqn. In 1939 he escaped to Poland. He was interned by the Soviets being released in 1941 and reached the United Kingdom. First operational posting No.313 (Czech) Sqn between October 1943 and May 1944. Posted to No.310 (Czech) Sqn, returning with this unit in Czechoslovakia in August 1945.
W/O : 9-44

PERNICA, Karel   W/O   (CZ)/RAF
2-44/2-45   RAF No.787387
                             RAF No.185293
Posted from No.410 R&SU. In 1939 he escaped to France via Poland. Enlisted in the *Armée de l' Air* but still under training when France collapsed. After the fall of France he reached the United Kingdom. Posted to No.310 (Czech) Sqn between December 1941 and July 1943. Second tour of operations with No.312 Sqn before being posted to No.310 Sqn again until the end of war.
P/O : 8-44

PEROUTKA, Stanislav   Sgt   (CZ)/RAF
9-40/10-42   RAF No.787705
                            RAF No.117372
Pre-war CzAF fighter pilot with Air Regiment 4. In June 1939 he escaped to France via Poland and enlisted in the *Armée de l' Air* on arrival. Posted to GC II/3

S. PEROUTKA

in December 1939, flying MS.406s and D.520s. Two confirmed victories, one being being shared with the French. Escaped to England. After retraining, became a founder member of the unit. Posted out in October 1942, tour expired. Another tour in February 1943 with No.310 Sqn until February 1945.
F/Sgt : 1-42

PIPA, Josef **   F/Sgt   (CZ)/RAF
6-41/11-42, 7-44/8-45 @   RAF No.787510
                      RAF No.145101
Posted from No.313 (Czech) Sqn. Pre-war CzAF pilot in Air Regiment 2. Escaped to France via Poland on 11.06.39. There, he enlisted in the Foreign Legion but when the war broke out he was transferred to the *Armée de l' Air* being posted to GC I/1 in March 1940 flying Blochs. Shared the destruction of a Do17 on 15.05.40. Sailed to England on 23.06.40. After retraining posted to No.43 Sqn (October 1940 - April 1941), and No.81 Sqn (April 1941 - May 1942), and eventually to No.313 (Czech) Sqn (May - June 1942). Ended his tour with the Squadron in November 1942. Returned to No.313 Sqn in February 1943 for another tour which ended in May 1944. Commissioned, he started another tour in July 1944 in No.310 (Czech) Sqn before being posted to No.312 Sqn as Flying Officer. In 1948 he emigrated to the United Kingdom and served again with the RAF. One shared confirmed victory with No.43 Sqn, Europe, 1941, one V-1, No.310 Sqn, 1944.
W/O : 10-42, F/L : 2-45

POPELKA, Viktor   F/Sgt   (CZ)/RAF
2-44/2-45   RAF No.787587
              RAF No.178523
Posted from RAF Croydon. Pre-war CzAF cadet under training when Czechoslovakia was occupied and escaped to France via Poland. Enlisted in the *Armée de l'Air* but did not complete his training. Escaped to England and completed his training. Posted to No.310 (Czech) Sqn in December 1941 remaining with it until the end of his tour in June 1943. Second tour of operations with No.312 Sqn and posted to No.310 Sqn one year later and returned to his country with it. One confirmed victory with No.310 Sqn, Europe, 1943.
W/O : 4-44

DFC : 14.02.45

POSLUZNY, Ondrej   P/O   (CZ)/RAF
9-40/9-40   RAF No.82568
Posted from No.310 (Czech) Sqn. He served as a pilot with the CzAF before the war. In 1939 he escaped to France. Served with the *Armée de l'Air* (GC III/4). On 28.06.40 he reached the United Kingdom. Retrained, he was posted to No.310 (Czech) Sqn in August until September and posted in, remaining only one week andg posted back to No.310 Sqn. In March 1941, he was posted to No.19 Sqn and to No.118 Sqn one week later and eventualy at the end of the month to No.32 Sqn.
†26.06.42, Hurricane IIB Z3088, No.32 Sqn, France.

V. POPELKA

Karel POSTA
RAF No.787624 (NCO)
RAF No.112546 (Officer)

Karel Posta was born in Plzen (Pilsen) on 29th September, 1914. He subsequently trained and became a skilled mechanical locksmith before enlisting in the CzAF. He was initially posted to *letecký pluk* 2 (Air Regiment 2) which was an observation wing. In 1937 he qualified as a fighter pilot and was posted to *stihaci letka* 34 (fighter flight No.34) of *letecký pluk* 1. On 12th May, 1939 he escaped to Poland, and on 25th June he was enrolled in the Czechoslovak consulate in Krakow. He then sailed to France where, after retraining, he was posted, on 15th May 1940, as a *caporal-chef* (Corporal) to *Groupe de Chasse* II/4, which was flying Curtiss H-75s. He scored for the first time on 9th June when he shared in the destruction of a He111. Two days later he shared in the destruction of a Hs126. He fought till 16th June 1940 by which time he had accumulated 30 hours of operational flying. He then retreated to Casablanca, Morocco and subsequently escaped to the United Kingdom where he arrived on 16th July 1940. He joined the RAF and on 19th September was posted to No.312 (Czechoslovak) Squadron as an NCO. During 1941 he took part in raids on targets across the Channel and in 1942 he was commissioned. During the Czechoslovak Wing's first combat, on 3rd June, he damaged two FW190s near Cherbourg. He finished his first tour on 1st March, 1943 and on 5th April he was posted to No.2 Delivery Flight in Colerne. Then he served at No.3501 Service Unit in Cranfield and before returning to operational flying he spent a week at Air Fighting Development Unit in Wittering where he flew a number of captured aircraft. He returned to No.312 Squadron, on 23rd June

1943, with the rank of Flying Officer. Shortly after his arrival the squadron moved to Scotland and on the evening of 27th August he, and Flight Lieutenant Karel Kasal, took off to intercept a reconnaissance Ju88. The fight lasted 20 minutes and at 18.50 hours their victim crashed into the North Sea. This was his last victory. Between 12th September and 2nd October he was at the Fighter Leaders School and on 15th November 1944 he returned to become the leader of A flight. His second tour ended on 17th February 1945. Posta was awarded the DFC, *Croix de Guerre*, Czech Military Cross (five times) and Medal for Bravery (three times). On 13th August he was one of the pilots who landed at Prague-Ruzyn airfield. After the war he served, with the rank of *Kapitan*, in 2.*letecka divize* (2nd Air Division) at Ceske Budejovice as the leader of *stíhací letka* (fighter flight) of 4th Air Regiment. His aerobatic displays were very popular but after the Communists coup he was dismissed from the army and returned to the United Kingdom. He rejoined the RAF with the rank of Sergeant and later reached the rank of Flight Lieutenant. He died of a heart attack on 8th January, 1961.

POSTA, Karel**   Sgt   (CZ)/RAF
9-40/3-43, 6-43/2-45   RAF No.787624
                     RAF No.112546

See biography. A Flight leader between 15.11.44 and
17.02.45, replacing V. Slouf. Replaced by A. Dvorak.
F/Sgt : 8-41, P/O :1-42

DFC : 14.02.45

J. PROKOPEC

POSTREHOVSKY, Bohumil   Sgt   (CZ)/RAF
7-41/10-41   RAF No.787488
Posted from No.52 OTU. Pre-war CzAF pilot. He
escaped to France via Poland and enlisted in the
Armée de l'Air on arrival. After retraining, served
with to GC I/8 (18.05.40), GC III/9 (01.06.40), GC
III/7 (06.06.40) and GC I/6 (17.06.40). Eventually he
reached the United Kingdom. Withdrawn from operations in October 1941.

PRISTUPA, Gustav   Sgt   (CZ)/RAF
7-44/8-44   RAF No.654758
Before the war he emmigrated to Canada. He enlisted
in the RAFVR but his previous postings are unknown.
On 11.08.44 he straffed a train near Arendonk,
Netherlands, but hit the trees and crashed. He survived,
suffering injuries but was captured by the Germans.
Liberated by the Red Army on 22.04.45.
F/Sgt : 7-44

17.11.41 he was posted in. Posted to No.57 OTU at the
end of his tour. Posted in for another tour in February
1944 from No.57 OTU as Warrant Officer. On 15.05.44
during the landing and taxiing on the airfield Manston he
collided with Spitfire flown by F/O Svetlik. He died of
wounds shortly after being taken to hospital.
F/Sgt : 10-42

PROKOPEC, Josef   F/Sgt   (CZ)/RAF
10-44/8-45 @   RAF No.788143
Posted from No.310 Sqn. In 1939 he escaped to
Poland. After 17.09.39 he was captured by the Soviets
and interned in USSR. Released, he arrived to
England in June 1941. Trained as fighter pilot and
posted to No.310 Sqn in January 1944.
W/O : 8-45

PRVONIC, Antonin   Sgt   (CZ)/RAF
11-41/6-43, 2-44/5-44 (†)   RAF No.788090
Slovak, posted from No.145 Sqn. Before the war he served in Air Regiment 3. When the Czechoslovak republic
was slipt into Slovak State and Protectorat *Böhmen und
Mähren*, he left the Air Force and he worked at guard of
finance of Slovak State. In October 1940 he escaped
from his country. He reached Palestina via Yugoslavia
and Turkey and enventually the United Kingdom in May
1941. Retrained, he was posted to No.145 Sqn in
September 1941 until November. Two months later, on

RICHTER, Karel   W/O   (cz)/RAF
9-41/10-41   RAF No.788029
Pre-war CzAF pilot. Escaped to Poland in July 1939
and joined the Polish Air Force, being eventually
captured by the Soviets. Released, he arrived in
England in October 1940. In July 1941 he was posted to No.43 Sqn and two months later posted to
No.312 Sqn, remaining only one month with it. In
January 1942, posted as pilot to No.24 Sqn, a
transport unit but in June, he was sent back to an
operational unit at the Czech flight of No.68 Sqn.
*†05.09.42, Beaufighter IF X7842, No.68 Sqn,
United Kingdom.*

ROHACEK, Rudolf   P/O   (CZ)/RAF
4-41/4-42 (†)   RAF No.81910
Posted from No.238 Sqn. Pre-war CzAF fighter pilot
with Air Regiment 4. On 27.06.39 he escaped to
France via Poland. He joined the *Armée de l'Air* but
saw no action. After the fall of France he went to the

United Kingdom and posted at once to No.310 (Czech) Sqn. Posted to No.6 OTU for retraining. Subsenquently, he was posted to No.601 Sqn in September 1940 and No.238 Sqn (October 1940 - April 1941). On 27.04.1942 he scrambled to intercept a lone Ju88. He crashed and perished near Axbridge, probably due of lost consciousness.
F/O : 8-41, F/L : 2-42

RUPRECHT, Vaclav   Sgt   (CZ)/RAF
7-41/4-43, 6-44/8-44 (†)   RAF No.787526
Posted from No.52 OTU. Under training in France in 1940, but evacuated before he could see any action. One tour of operations with the Squadron and posted to No.2 DF at the end of his first tour. Another tour with No.313 (Czech) Sqn between October 1943 and May 1944 before returning to No.312 Sqn in June as Warrant Officer. On 25.08.1944 he failed to return from the sortie type *Ranger*.
F/Sgt : 10-42

SAMBERGER, Ondrej   Sgt   (CZ)/RAF
12-44/2-45 (†)   RAF No.787806
Posted from No.57 OTU. Killed during the training flight, probably due of failure of the oxygen system.
F/Sgt : 1-45

V. SLOUF

SKACH, Antonin   W/O   (CZ)/RAF
2-44/7-44   RAF No.788032
Posted from No.18 APC. Pre-war pilot of CzAF with Air Regiment 1. In 1939 he escaped to Poland but in September he was interned by the Red Army. Released, he arrived to the United Kingdom in October 1940. For a short time, he served with No.2 SS and in May 1941 he was sent to flying school to be retrained. In July 1941 posted to No.1 Sqn, and to No.310 (Czech) Sqn in September in which he remained at the end of his tour in June 1943. Posted in for another tour in February 1944. Posted to No.310 Sqn for the second time in July 1944.
†03.09.44, Spitfire IX MJ311, No.310 Sqn, United Kingdom.

SKRINAR, Jan   Sgt   (CZ)/RAF
7-44/8-45 @   RAF No.787887
Slovak posted from Czech Depot serving with the unit until the end of war.
F/Sgt : 10-44, W/O : 2-45

SLOUF, Karel   Sgt   (CZ)/RAF
4-45/8-45 @   RAF No.787706
Posted from No.57 OTU. Former armourer with the Squadron before being accepted to a pilot course. Vaclav Slouf's brother.

SLOUF, Vaclav ***   Sgt   (CZ)/RAF
9-40/6-42, 8-42/2-44, 10-44/4-45   RAF No.787706
                       RAF No.112547
Pre-war CzAF pilot with Air Regiment 3. Escaped to France via Poland on 08.06.39, enlisting in the *Armée de l'Air* in September. Posted to GC III/3 in December flying MS.406s and D.520s. In May - June 1940 he claimed three confirmed victories, two being shared, but was shot down once. In June he retreated to North Africa and evacuated to England. Retrained, he became a founder member of the Squadron and was posted to No.53 OTU at the end of his tour. Returned to the Squadron in August from No.52 OTU. On 01.07.43 he was appointed commander of B flight, replacing V. Kaslik. End of his tour on 01.02.44 relinquishing B flight to V. Smolik and went to Czechoslovak Air Ministry in London. Third tour of operations serving with No.313 (Czech) Sqn between May and October 1944, before being posted in again as A Flight leader, replacing J. Keprt. When he became the CO the Squadron, he was replaced by K. Posta. Posted to CIG until the end of war. After the

O.SMIK

war he served at 2nd Air Division of CzAF. Demobilised in 1946, became an airline pilot with CSA, but after Communist coup he emigrated to the United Kingdom serving again the RAF.

DFC : 05.11.45

SMIK, Otto*   P/O   (CZ)/RAF
1-43/1-43, 7-44/9-44   RAF No.130678

Slovak. Posted from No.310 (Czech) Sqn, with which he stayed two days only. Born in Georgia, Soviet Union from a Slovak father, and Russian mother. Glider pilot before the war. On 18.03.40 he escaped to France via Hungary. In June 1940 he arrived to the Czechoslovak depot in Adge but saw no action. Evacuated to the United Kingdom and enlisted to the RAF in July 1940. His first stay in No.312 Sqn was short as he was posted to No.131 Sqn one week after his arrival and in March he was posted to No.122 Sqn until May. Then, posted to No.222 (Natal) Sqn until December when his tour expired. Second tour of operations from March 1944 with No.310 Sqn again until July 1944. Posted to No.312 Sqn as Fllight Lieutenant to lead B flight replacing V. Smolik from 11.07.44 onwards. On 03.09.44 he was shot down by *flak*, B flight being taken over to J. Sodek. He managed to evade capture, returning to England on 29.10.44. In November 1944, became CO of No.127 Sqn. Ten confirmed victories, two being sha-

red, with Nos.122, 222 and 310 Sqn, Europe, 1943 - 1944, three V-1s, No.310 Sqn. DFC [No.222 Sqn]. *†28.11.44, Spitfire XVI RR227, CO No.127 Sqn, Netherlands.*

SMOLIK, Vojtech*   Sgt   (CZ)/RAF
9-40/9-42, 12-43/7-44   RAF No.787708
                                  RAF No.117369

See biography. B flight leader between 01.02.44 and 11.07.44. He was replacing V. Slouf. At his departure, he was replaced by O. Smik.
F/Sgt : 1-42, P/O: 3-42, F/L : 2-44

DFC : 14.02.45

SMOLKA, Erich   W/O   (CZ)/RAF
10-44/8-45 @   RAF No.787045
                                  RAF No.186715

Posted from No.310 (Czech) Sqn. Pre-war CzAF pilot. In 1939 he escaped to France and was posted to Czechoslovak Depot at Adge but saw no action. Evacuated to the United Kingdom. With No.313 (Czech) Sqn between March 1943 and June 1944. In October 1944 he was posted to No.310 Sqn and a week later to No.312 Sqn.
P/O : 11-44, F/O : 4-45

SODEK, Jaroslav*   Sgt   (CZ)/RAF
6-41/8-41, 9-41/9-42, 4-43/2-45   RAF No.787426
                                  RAF No.146372

Posted from No.258 Sqn. Pre-war CzAF pilot with Air Regiment 2. He escaped to France via Poland on 20.06.39. Enlisted in the *Armée de l' Air* being posted to ELD Chartres in May 1940 at the completion of his training subsenquently to GC III/9 and GC III/7. On 17.06.40 he was posted to the Czech *escadrille* at GC I/6. After the fall of France he escaped to the United Kingdom. In October 1940 posted to No.32 Sqn and the following month to No.258 Sqn. Posted in for two months before being posted to No.1 Sqn but returned to the Squadron the following month. Posted out at the end of his tour serving with a delivery flight. Posted to No.286 Sqn and No.2 DF between March 1943 and April 1943 before returning to the Squadron. B flight leader between 03.09.44, after O.Smik had been shot down and 01.02.45 relinquishing command to J.Pipa when his tour ended and posted to No.41 OTU. He returned to Czechoslovakia and remained with the new CzAF.

Vojtech SMOLIK
RAF No.787708 (NCO)
RAF No.117369 (Officer)

Vojtech Smolik was born on 22nd September, 1916 in the Besednice district Cesky Krumlov. After he had completed eight classes of basic education he moved to the Secondary Technical School. Subsequently he worked as a technician clerk then, in 1936 and 1937, he trained as a pilot at *letecky pluk* 4 (Air Regiment 4). Smolik was posted to *letecky pluk* 6 on 1st June 1937 where his flying skills resulted in him being transferred to the aerobatic team led by Frantisek Novak, the leader of *stihaci letka* 44 (fighter flight 44). This nine man team flew Avia Ba-122s and while training for the festivities of the Sokol a strong gust of wind caused three aircraft to collide on 23rd June. Sergeant Smolik managed to bale out but Rudolf Motycka and Vlastimil Rys were killed. The flypast on 6th July 1938, which opened the festivities, was a successful and innovative performance. After the *Protektorat Böhmen und Mähren* was established he escaped to Poland on 24th April 1939 and in June he arrived in France and was posted to Sidi-bel-Abbes to join the *Legion Etrangère*. He trained as an infantryman then when war broke out he was posted to Marrakesh, Morocco, and then to Blida, Tunisia, for flying training. In November he arrived in Tunis and trained as a fighter pilot and was promoted to the rank of Sergeant. On 1st November, 1939 he was transferred to the *Escadrille Régionale de Chasse* (ERC) 572 at Bizerte-Sidi Ahmed which was still flying Blériot-SPAD 510s but shortly afterwards its first MS 406s were delivered. *Groupe de Chasse* GC III/5 was established on 15th May, 1940 and transferred to Bir-Guenich on 28th May. When Italy entered into the war GC III/5 fought against the Regia Aeronautica but Smolik's combats against the Italians are not recorded.

After the fall of France he escaped, via Gibraltar, to Great Britain, joined the RAF and on 19th September, 1940 was posted to No.312 Squadron with the rank of Sergeant as funder member. On 5th July, 1941 he gained his first success in the air, a probably destroyed Bf109, over Lille. Three days later, during *Circus* 39, the Kenley Wing escorted Stirlings to Lens and Smolik claimed another Bf109. On 19th December 1941 he collided during the mock fight with a Spitfire flown by Sergeant Jaroslav Kucera and while he managed to bale out Kucera was killed. In 1942 Smolik was commissioned and in August took part in the Operation *Jubilee*. During the second sortie on 19th August he damaged a FW190. Shortly afterwards he finished his first tour and was promoted to the rank of Flying Officer. On 16th December he rejoined the Squadron and on 1st February 1944 he became B flight's leader. He finished his second tour on 12th July and was sent on a course to become a flying instructor. He then served at the flying school in Spitalgate until March 1945 when he was transferred to No.313 (Czechoslovak) Squadron. On 25th March he passed the leaving examination at the Czechoslovak Secondary Grammar School in Llanwrtyd in Wales. For his war service he was awarded the Czechoslovak Military Cross, on three occasions, and the DFC. In July 1945 he returned to his country but after the events in February 1948 he again escaped to the United Kingdom and rejoined the RAF. Smolik died on 7th August, 1991.

O. SPACEK

But after the Communist coup he emigrated to the United Kingdom and rejoined the RAF.
F/Sgt : 1-42, W/O : 5-42, P/O : 4-43, F/O : 12-43, F/L : 9 -44.

SOUKUP, Vladimir　　　Sgt　　(CZ)/RAF
5-43/7-44　　　　　　　RAF No.787409
Posted from No.57 OTU. After the occupation of his country he escaped to France. There he was posted to Czechoslovak Depot in Adge. Subsequenty he escaped to United Kingdom and enlisted in the RAF. Posted to No.310 (Czech) Sqn until January 1945 when his tour expired.
F/Sgt : 11-43

SPACEK, Otto　　　Sgt　　(CZ)/RAF
10-40/5-41　　　　　　RAF No.787671
Pre-war CzAF member with Air Regiment 3. After occupation of country in 1939 he escaped to France via Poland. Entered into the *Armée de l' Air* and after retraining on French fighters he was posted to GC I/8 equipped by MB.152 in March 1940. Two confirmed victories with the French one being shared in May and June 1940, but shot down twice, being slightly injurned each time. Evacuated to England and posted in after his retraining. Posted to No.615 Sqn before being posted to No.313 (Czech) Sqn in June 1941 serving with this uniti until the end of war.

Commissioned in 1944. After the Communist coup, he emigrated, returning to Czech Republic in 1993.

STANC, Alois　　　Sgt　　(CZ)/RAF
6-44/8-45 @　　　　　　RAF No. 787791
Posted from No.53 OTU. Former Squadron's ground crew accepted for a pilot course.
F/Sgt : 7-44, P/O : 6-45

STANDERA, Miroslav　　　Sgt　　(CZ)/RAF
10-40/8-42, 1-43/8-43　　　RAF No.787626
Posted from No.6 OTU. Pre-war member of CzAF still under training when the Country was occupied. Escaped to France via Poland on 01.06.39 and joined the *Armée de l' Air*. Served with ELD Chartres before being posted to GC II/10 and in June he was posted to GC I/6. On 26.06.1940 he was evacuated to the United Kingdom. Posted out in August 1942 when he completed his tour and posted to No.43 Group for rest. Returned to the Squadron in January 1943 until August the same year. Retrained on twin-engined aircraft, he was posted to the Czech flight of No.68 Sqn in February 1944 until March 1945, having received his commission meanwhile. He remained with the new CzAF, serving with 24 *bombardovaci pluk* (Bomber Regiment 24). After the Communist coup he emigrated.
F/Sgt : 4-42

STASTNY, Jan　　　P/O　　(CZ)/RAF
1-43/10-43 (†)　　　　　RAF No.125415
Posted from No.61 OTU. Pre-war CzAF pilot serving with Air Regiment 4. In 1941 he was accepted into the Air Force of the Red Army (VVS - *Voenno-vozdushnye sily*). He was a flying instructor in a Fighter Centre of the South Front and later he served at 246th Air Fighter Regiment (246th IAP). In March 1942 he was included into the group of Czechoslovak pilots and sailed on board of HMS *Edinburgh*. However the cruiser was sunk but he was rescued. On 15th May he survived the sunk of HMS *Trinidad*, and reached Iceland and subsequently United Kingdom. After the retraining on British planes he was posted to No.312 Sqn in January 1943. Hit by *flak* during *Ramrod* 95, and bailed out but drowned in the waters of Channel.
F/O : 5-43

STEFAN, Jan　　　F/Sgt　　(CZ)/RAF
11-42/2-43　　　　　　RAF No.787599

Posted from RAF Harrowbeer. Pre-war CzAF Pilot. He escaped to France and joined the *Armée de l' Air*. After retraining on French planes he was posted to GC I/10 in May 1940. After the fall of France evacuated to the United Kingdom and after being retrained he was posted to No.1 Sqn between October 1940 and July 1941, No.65 Sqn between July and April 1942, No.313 (Czech) Sqn for one week in April 1942 before returning the same month to No.1 Sqn and ending his tour in July 1942. Posted in for another tour in November 1942 until February 1943. being posted to No.310 (Czech) Sqn until March. No more operational postings until the end of war. After the Communist coup in 1948 he emigrated to the UK, later moving to Canada.

STEHLIK, Josef   Sgt   (CZ)/RAF
9-40/10-41, 4-43/1-44   RAF No.787701
                              RAF No.104693

Pre-war CzAF member, first as engineer before being accepted for a pilot course serving with Air Regiment 3. Escaped from his country on 05.06.39 and when he arrived in France he enlisted in the *Armée de l'Air* in October that year. From December 1939 onwards, he served with GC III/3, on Moranes first, later on Dewoitines. Escaped to the UK in July 1940 and posted in after the completion of his training. Posted to Central Flying School in October 1941. Served as flying instructor in Canada for one year being back to the Squadron in April 1943. Volunteered to serve on the Eastern Front, he was discharged from the RAF on 01.02.44. Served with 1ˢᵗ Czechoslovak Fighter Regiment and the new formed 2ⁿᵈ Czechoslovak Fighter Regiment in November 1944 onwards. Remained with the new CzAF, and despite his service with the Soviets in 1944 -1945, he was persecuted after February 1948, put into jail for seven months, and turned out from the Air Force, working as labourer the following years. Ten confirmed victories, with the French, Battle of France, 1940, No.312 Sqn, Battle of Britain, 1940 and Europe, 1941, 1ˢᵗ Cz Regiment, Europe, 1944.
P/O : 8-41, F/L : 8-43

STEINER, Frantisek   Sgt   (CZ)/RAF
10-44/8-45 @   RAF No.788107
Posted from No.313 (Czech) Sqn in which he was serving for six weeks.
F/Sgt : 10-44

STICKA, Frantisek   Sgt   (CZ)/RAF
6-41/8-41, 9-41/8-42, 1-43/2-44   RAF No.787585
                              RAF No.158966

Posted from No.258 Sqn. Pre-war CzAF pilot in Air Regiment 4. On 06.06.1939 he escaped to France via Poland and enlisted in the *Armée de l' Air*. After retraining, he was posted to GC I/4 flying Curtisses. Wounded in action on 06.06.40. Retreated to North Africa and then evacuated to the United Kingdom. Joined the RAF. Retrained at No.6 OTU and posted to No.32 Sqn in October before being posted to No.258 Sqn the following month. Posted in June 1941 but posted to No.1 Sqn in August returning to the Squadron in September remaining in until the end of his tour in August 1942 and posted to No.43 Group for rest. Posted in again in January 1943 for another tour as Warrant Officer. Volunteered to serve in Soviet Union, was discharged from RAF on 01.02.44 and became a member of 1ˢᵗ Czechoslovak Air Fighter Regiment. He saw action over Slovakia in September and October 1944. In 1945 he was posted to new 2ⁿᵈ Czechoslovak Air Fighter Regiment. After the war with the new Czechoslovak Air Force but in 1948 he emigrated and again rejoining again the RAF.
F/Sgt : 5-42, P/O : 9-43

SVETLIK, Ladislav   Sgt   (CZ)/RAF
9-40/8-42, 1-43/7-44   RAF No.787700
                              RAF No.117371

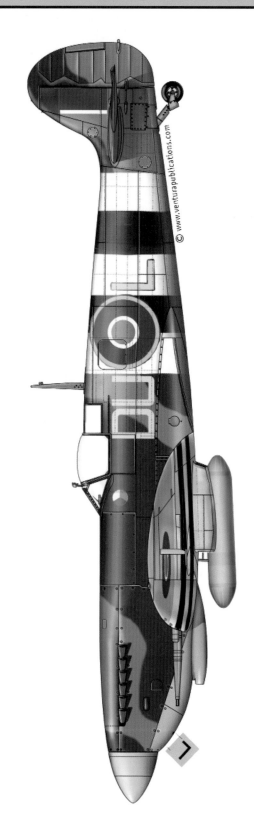

Supermarine Spitfire LF.IXC MJ840, No.312 (Czechoslovak) Squadron, Flight Lieutenant L. Svetlik, Appledram, June 1944.

L. SVETLIK

I. TONDER

Pre-war CzAF pilot with Air Regiment 3. Escaped to France on 10.06.39 and joined the *Armée de l'Air* on arrival. With GC II/5 between December 1939 and June 1940. Five shared confirmed victories with the French. Reached Great Britain and joined the RAF and posted in as founder member of the Squadron completed his tour in August 1942. Returned to the Squadron for another tour in January 1943 as Flying Officer. In November 1944 he was sent to No.105 (T) OTU to become a transport pilot serving in 1945 at No.11 Ferry Unit and No.147 Sqn. In August he returned to Czechoslovakia and served with the Air Transport Group, at Prague-Ruzyne, which was commanded by Jan Klan, another No.312 Squadron pilot. In 1946 he joined CSA, the national airline, as a captain. Four years later, on 24.03.50, fearing persecution from the Communists, he took part in the escape of several former RAF pilots. He flew Dakota OK-WDR from Ostrava and, instead of landing at Prague-Ruzyne, carried on to Erding near Munich. He re-enlisted in the RAF with the rank of Flying Officer and served in Great Britain, Malta and Far East before retiring in 1966 as the Station Commander RAF Theddlethorpe. He initially settled in Malta and, in 1973, moved to New Zealand. One confirmed victory, No.312 Sqn, Europe, 1944.
F/Sgt : 1-42, P/O : 3-42, F/L : 2-44

TESINSKY, Josef   P/O   (CZ)/RAF
2-45/8-45@   RAF No.89733
Posted from No.57 OTU. No more details available.
F/O : 4-45

TOCAUER, Stanislav   Sgt   (CZ)/RAF
2-42/5-43   RAF No.788044
Posted from No.52 OTU. Pre-war CzAF member under training when the country was occupied. Escaped on 24.05.40 to the United Kingdom via Hungary, Yugoslavia and Palestine. Posted in for the duration of his first tour at the completion of his training. Posted to No.1 Delivery Flight. Another tour with No.310 (Czech) Sqn between November 1943 and February 1944 when he volunteered to serve in Soviet Union and was discharged from RAF. On the Eastern Front he served with 1st Czechoslovak Air Fighter Regiment and took part in the combats over Slovakia in September and October, later serving with the 2nd Czechoslovak Air Fighter Regiment as an instructor.
F/Sgt : 10-42

TONDER, Ivo   P/O   (CZ)/RAF
10-40/6-42   RAF No.83232
Posted from No.6 OTU. Pre-war CzAF pilot with Air Regiment 1. After March 1939 he worked as a designer at the factory Aero but in December he escaped to France via Hungary, Yugoslavia, Greece, Turkey, Syria and Lebanon. In March 1940 he was posted to Czechoslovak Depot in Adge. After the fall of France he was evacuated to the United Kingdom. On 03.06.42 he failed to return from *Circus* 6, being shot down by FW190s. He bailed out and fell into the captivity. He was posted to the prisoner camp *Stalag Luft III* in Sagan. He took part in the Great Escape in the night 24-25.03.44 but re-captured on 30th March but avoided execution by

the *Gestapo*. On 30.11.44 relocated to *Stalag Luft I* in Barth and on 08.01.45 sent to *Oflag IV* in Colditz. Liberated on 16.04.45. On 29.06.45 he was posted to No.313 Sqn. In 1947 he was demobilized, however he was arrested soon after. In November 1949 he managed to escape to Austria and settled in Great Britain.

TRUHLAR, Frantisek P/O (CZ)/RAF
9-43/6-44 RAF No.89643
Posted from No.57 OTU. Pre-war member of CzAF still under training when the Czechoslovakia was occupied. Arrived in England during Summer 1940 and in August was posted to No.311 (Czech) sqn as air gunner and Pilot Officer. Severely wounded in a Wellington crash on 17.10.40 and returning to his unit in November 1941 only, and asked to become a fighter pilot. Posted in at the completion of his training. Injurned in a Spitfire crash on 11.06.44 and did not return to Squadron. After the recovery he continued to serve the new CzAF but was killed in flying accident on 03.12.1946 (Spitfire TE562).

TRUHLAR, Jan Sgt (CZ)/RAF
9-40/7-41 RAF No.787508
Pre-war CzAF pilot with Air Regiment 1. After March 1939 he decided with his brother Vaclav to escape from Czechoslovakia, crossing the boundary to Poland on 01.06.39, and heading to France to join the *Armée de l' Air*. After retraining, he was posted to GC II/4 in December 1939, flying Curtisses. Two confirmed victories with the French, one being shared. After the fall of France he was evacuated to the United Kingdom and enlisted in the RAF. Founder member of the Squadron. Shot down during *Circus* 41 and became a PoW on 09.07.41. During the transport to *Stalag IXC* in Bad Sulza he twice escaped but was recaptured and posted to *Stalag XIIIB*. Then sent to *Stalag IXC* and subsequently to *Stalag Luft III* in Sagan and later to *Stalag Luft I* in Barth. On 16 April 1945 he was liberated in the *Oflag IVC* in Colditz. He was commissioned and posted to No.313 (Czech) Sqn for the return to Czechoslovakia. After the war he served with the new CzAF but eventually was turned out from the Air Force in February 1949.

TYSON, Frank H.* S/L RAF
8-40/4-41 RAF No.26248
Posted from No.3 Sqn. Pre-war RAF regular officer, having served with No.603 Squadron, AuxAF in 1937 -

1939. First CO No.245 Sqn at the formation of the unit in October 1939, leaving the unit the following month. To gain combat experience, he was posted as supernumerary Squadron Leader to No.3 Sqn in August 1940 and posted in September. Posted to No.1 Polish F.T.C in April. No more operational postings until the end of war, serving at Malta in 1942. Remained with the RAF after the war retiring as Group Captain in 1962.
W/C : 3-41

VACULIK, Frantisek Sgt (cz)/RAF
4-42/5-42 RAF No.787378
Pre-war CzAF member until training in 1939. He escaped to France and posted to Czechoslovak Depot in Adge. After the fall of France evacuated to the United Kingdom and completed his training. Posted in April 1942. Badly Injurned at the head in flying accident on 02.05.42. After recovery, posted to No.310 (Czech) Sqn between April 1943 and February 1943. Volunteered for a service in Soviet Union, he was discharged from RAF. Became a member of 1ˢᵗ Cz Fighter Regiment.
†20.09.44, La5-FN No.151, 1ˢᵗ Cz Fighter Regiment, Slovakia.

VANCL, Frantisek* F/L (CZ)/RAF
10-43/5-44 RAF No.87628

F. VANCL

A. VANKO

In 1933 he entered into the Cz Army, as infantryman before becoming a fighter pilot in Air Regiment 1. On 28.05.39 he escaped to France via Poland. Joined the *Armée de l' Air* and in January 1940 he was posted to GC I/7 in Syria. After the Armistice he escaped to Egypt and subsequently to Great Britain. Posted to No.313 (Czech) Sqn between September 1941 and May 1942, and to No.129 Sqn until August when he was posted to No.111 Sqn for a short stay, but was posted to No.611 Sqn at the end of the same month remaining in until the end of his tour in January 1943. Another tour with No.312 Sqn in October and became the CO one week later. Posted to HQ of No.11 Group as a liaison officer of Czechoslovak Inspectorat. After the war he continued serving the new CzAF. He was the commander of 1ˢᵗ Air Division but after Communist coup he escaped and joined the RAF for a second time. One confirmed victory, No.129 Sqn, Europe, 1942.
S/L : 10-43

VANKO, Anton   Sgt   (CZ)/RAF
11-44/12-44 (†)   RAF No.788644
Slovak, posted from No.57 OTU. He served with the Slovakian State Air Force but on 18.04.1943 he flew over with licence-built bomber Avia B-71 to Turkey. He reached the United Kingdom via Syria, Palestine and Egypt to joined the RAF. On 08.12.44 during the taxiing to escort of Lancasters, *Ramrod* 1401, his Spitfire colli-

ded with Skrinar's plane and could not escape from the burning aircraft.

VASATKO, Alois***   P/O   (CZ)/RAF
9-40/4-42   RAF No.83233
See biography. Fully B flight leader on 10.04.41, succeeding A.M. Dawbarn. When he became CO of the Squadron on 05.06.41, he was replaced by T. Vybiral.
F/L : 12-40, S/L : 7-41

DFC : 01.07.42

VAVRIK, Josef   Sgt   (CZ)/RAF
4-45/8-45 @   RAF No.787520
Posted from No.57 OTU. Former armourer with the Squadron before being accepted for a pilot course.
F/Sgt : 6-45

VAVRINEK, Frantisek   W/O   (CZ)/RAF
11-43/5-44   RAF No.788157
      RAF No.174310
Posted from No.61 OTU. Pre-war CzAF pilot with Air Regiment 3. In June 1939 he escaped to Poland and on 29.08.39 he enlisted in the Polish Air Force, being later interned by Red Army. Released in February 1941 he set out from Odessa to Istanbul. Later he was included into the Czechoslovak Army in the Middle East but soon sailed to England in May 1941 to join the RAF. Posted to No.313 (Czech) Sqn on completion of his training in March 1942 until May 1943. Posted in for another tour and posted to No.84 GSU at the end of his tour. Last tour with No.313 Sqn again between July 1944 and the end of war.
P/O : 3-44

VELLA, Jan   Sgt   (CZ)/RAF
10-40/3-41   RAF No.787677
Posted from No.6 OTU. Pre-war CzAF pilot with Air Regiment 3 where he served until 1928 for his military service. He was demobilized and worked as engine-driver at state railway. On 06.11.39 he escaped to France via Hungary, Romania and Lebanon arriving in France in December. He was posted to Air Group of Czechoslovak Depot in Adge. After the fall of France he was evacuated to the United Kingdom. In March 1941 he was taken from operations due to his age (he was born in 1906). Then he flew as a test pilot at different Maintenance Units. In January 1943 he was posted to No.6 (Coastal) OTU and in April posted to No.311

Alois VASATKO
RAF No.83233

Born on 25th August 1908 in Celakovice, Czechoslovakia, he was the son of a joiner, one of five children. His father became an invalid so he was brought up by his uncle in Litohrady near Rychnov nad Kneznou. In 1928 he was called up for military service. He liked the experience and decided to become a professional soldier and attended the Military Academy. In 1931 he graduated as Lieutenant of artillery and, after having served in two artillery Regiments, was posted to the air observers school and on 31st December 1936 he was transferred to the air force. In 1937 - 1938 he completed his flying training and became the leader of *pozorovaci letka* 14 (Observation Flight 14), which was equipped with Letov S-328s, with the rank of 1st lieutenant. When mobilisation took place in September 1938 his unit was ordered to co-operate with the 2nd Field Army. After the German occupation he escaped to Poland on 9th July 1939 and on 28th July sailed to France. On 7th September he joined the *Armée de l' Air* and was posted to CIC (Fighter OTU) in Chartres. He was promoted to the rank of captain on 1st May 1940 and on 11th May was transferred to GC I/5 flying Curtiss H-75s. He claimed his first success, against a Bf109, during a patrol on 17th May when the French unit shot down two of these aircraft, Vasatko shared both victories. In the next few weeks his tally rose to twelve confirmed victories and two probable, all but two of these being confirmed as shared. He was injured in combat once during the Battle for France.

On 21st June he flew to Algeria, on 4th July he was awarded the *Légion d' Honneur* and on 9th July he set out to make his way to England, via Morocco and Gibraltar. There on 16th August he joined the RAF with the rank of Pilot Officer and on 5th September 1940 he was posted to No.312 Squadron as founder member. He shared the squadron's first victory together with F/Lt D.E. Gillam

and Sgt Stehlik. Three days later he engaged in combat with a Do17, five pilots fired all their ammunition at this aircraft and made several hits on the bomber, however this claim was not confirmed. Next month he was promoted to the rank of Flight Lieutenant and was named the Czechoslovak leader of B Flight. When the squadron was included in the Kenley Wing, late in May, he took part in the offensive raids on targets in France and Belgium. On 5th June he was promoted to Squadron Leader and took over the command of the Squadron. On 9th July 1941, during *Circus* 41, he claimed one Bf109 probably destroyed and another damaged. In August he sent the Inspectorat of Czechoslovak Air Ministry a proposal to establish a Czechoslovak fighter wing. He was an untiring and zealous proponent of this unit. On 1st May 1942 his dream became a reality and he was promoted to the rank of Wing Commander and soon after the squadron moved to the Exeter Sector. On 7th May, Nos.310 and 154 Squadrons arrived to complete the Exeter Wing. On 1st June the Czechoslovak Wing carried out *Ramrod* 12, its first operation. Two days he claimed one FW190 as probably destroyed but the wing lost three pilots. On 8th June No.313 Squadron arrived to replace No.154 Squadron and Vasatko had all three Czechoslovak fighter squadrons under his command. In the evening of 23rd June he took off with the Wing on *Ramrod* 23. During the return flight the formation was attacked by FW190s of III./JG 2 near the Isle of Batz. Alois Vasatko gave his last order and then turned towards the enemy fighters but his plane collided with a FW190 and failed to bail out he drowned in the Channel. The award of a DFC was gazetted the following month to add to the French *Croix de Guerre* with five palmes and four stars, which he had received from the French. He had also the Czech War Cross with two Bars.

Sqn. In October 1943 he was commissioned. DFC [No.311 (Czech) Sqn].
†10.01.45, Oxford I PH404, No.311 (Czech) Sqn, United Kingdom.

A. VRANA

VESELY, Vlastimil   P/O   (CZ)/RAF
9-40/2-41   RAF No.83234

Pre-war CzAF pilot with Air Regiment 4. In 1937 he became a fighter pilot and later being graduated as night fighter pilot. On 18.05.39 he escaped to France via Poland to join the *Armée de l' Air*. On completion of his training he was posted to GC I/9 in March 1940. On 17.06.40 he claimed the destruction of an Italian SM.79, but this victory was later downgraded as probable destroyed. After the Armistice he was evacuated to England and after being retrained, became a founder member of the Squadron. Posted to No.96 night fighter Sqn, remaining until August. Posted to Czech flight of No.68 Sqn between December 1941 and April 1943, leading the Czech flight from January 1942 onwards. In October, he returned to No.68 Sqn until January 1944 before being called back to CIG. After the war he continued to serve the new CzAF, commanding Bomber Regiment 24. However he emigrated after Comminst coup and rejoined the RAF. Two confirmed victories, one being shared, No.68 Sqn, Europe, 1943. DFC [No.68 Sqn].

VONDRACEK, Frantisek   Sgt   (CZ)/RAF
7-43/7-43   RAF No.787370

Not much details available on this pilot who remained with the Squadron one week only. He was discharged from RAF in November 1943.

VOTRUBA, Bohumil   Sgt   (CZ)/RAF
9-40/5-41 (†)   RAF No.787435

Pre-war CzAF pilot. In 1939 he escaped to France and joined the *Armée de l' Air*. After retraining on French fighters he was posted to GC I/10 six days after the German offensive. After the fall of France he reached Great Britain and became a founder member of the Squadron. During a night patrol base, he got lost and run out of fuel. Baled out too low and was killed.

**VRANA, Adolf ***   P/O   (CZ)/RAF
9-40/7-41, 6-42/6-43   RAF No.83235

Pre-war CzAF ground mechanic and pilot. Escaped to France via Poland on 31.07.39 and enlisted in the *Armée de l' Air* on arrival. On 11.05.40 he was posted to GC I/5 flying Curtiss H-75s. Shot down once, but shared two confirmed victories during the Campaign. After the fall of France he escaped to the United Kingdom. Founder member of the Squadron. Posted out as ferry pilot for rest. After three months he was posted to No.310 Sqn as a Flying Control Officer and three months later posted back to the Unit for the same duty. In June 1942 he became again an operational pilot. Became twice B flight leader, the first time betweeen 25.08.42 and 29.09.42 replacing K. Kasal and the second time on 01.01.43 when T. Vybiral took command of the Squadron. When he ended his tour on 01.06.43, he was replaced by V. Kaslik. After the war he continued to serve with CzAF. But after the communist coup he emigrated to United Kingdom and between 1950 and 1961 rejoined the RAF.
F/O : 1-41, F/L : 12-41

**VYBIRAL, Tomas ***   P/O   (CZ)/RAF
9-40/6-42, 11-42/11-43   RAF No.83236

Pre-war CzAF pilot serving with Air Regiment 3, escaping from his country on 18.06.39. On arrival in France he enlisted in the *Armée de l'Air*, becoming operational with GC I/5 on 11.05.40. During the Battle of France he claimed seven victories, six of them were shared. He retreated with his unit to North Africa, and from there reached England via Gibraltar in August 1940. Posted in as founder member after being retrained by the RAF. Posted to No.2 DF at the end of his first tour, returning in November 1942 for another tour which ended one

T. VYBIRAL

year later. He was B flight leader between 15.11.42 and 01.01.43, replacing K. Kasal. Replaced by A. Vrana. In February 1944, he took command of No.134 (Czech) Wing, remaining at the head of this Wing until November 1944. Remained with the new CzAF after the war, but escaped to the United Kingdom once again in September 1948 after the Communist coup. DSO [No.134 (Czech) Wing], DFC [No.19 Sector].
F/O : 1-41, F/L : 12-41

VYCHODIL, Oldrich F/Sgt (CZ)/RAF
11-42/4-44 RAF No.787375
Posted from No.61 OTU. Pre-war CzAF pilot, but no more details are available. Posted to No.84 GSU in April 1944. One tour with No.312 Sqn, another with No.313 Sqn between July 1944 and end of war. Commissioned during the war.
W/O : 1-43

YOUNG, John R.C. F/O RAF
10-40/10-40 RAF No.70766
Posted from No.249 Sqn. Pre-war RAF pilot, serving as flying instructor with No.41 Sqn, and its satellite AuxAF squadrons, Nos.603 and 609. In October, he was posted as fighter pilot to No.603 Sqn before becoming a founder member of No.249 Sqn in May 1940. Remaining one week only with the Squadron, he later served with two Polish units No.308 Sqn (November 1940 - March 1941), and No.317 Sqn (March - April

1941), and eventually with No.406 (RCAF) Sqn in April 1941. Also CO No.289 Sqn and No.108 Sqn (July 1944 - Februry 1945). Returned to his Reserve status in April 1945. AFC [01.01.42].

ZAKRAVSKY, Jindrich Sgt (CZ)/RAF
9-42/4-44 RAF No.787546
Posted from No.61 OTU. Pre-war CzAF pilot. In 1940 he reached Great Britain. After retraining posted to No.24 Sqn. Posted in for a full tour which ended in May 1944. Posted first to No.420 R&S Unit he then was posted No.667 squadron (Army Co-operation Unit).
F/Sgt : 5-43, W/O : 2-44
†26.09.44, Hurricane IIC LF756, No.667 Sqn, United Kingdom.

ZALESKY, Alois P/O (CZ)/RAF
2-45/2-45 (†) RAF No.185292
Posted from Gatwick. Under training in France, but saw no action. Served with No.313 (Czech) Sqn between April 1943 and July 1944 before to be posted to No.310 (Czech) where he remained three weeks only. Posted in for a second tour. Killed in flying accident.
F/O : 2-45

ZARECKY, Jindrich Sgt (CZ)/RAF
6-44/8-45 @ RAF No.787107
Posted from No.84 GSU. Former ground crew serving with No.310 (Czech) Sqn. Accepted for a pilot training. Served with the new CzAF but after the Communist coup he emigrated and joined again the RAF. He was killed in board of the Beverley C.1 XH117 which crashed on 05.03.57. He was a passenger.
F/Sgt : 10-44

ZAVORAL, Antonin Sgt (CZ)/RAF
4-41/10-41 RAF No.787660
Posted from No.1 Sqn. Pre-war CzAF pilot. In 1939 he managed to escape to France and joined the *Armée de l' Air*. On 20.05.40, he was posted to ELD Chartres. One confirmed victory with the French, a Do17 on 11.06.40. After the fall of France he was evacuated to the United Kingdom. In early October 1940 he was posted to No.1 Sqn until April 1941. Posted to No.607 Sqn, being killed a couple of days later. One confirmed victory, No.312 Sqn, Europe, 1941.
†31.10.41, Hurricane IIB BE403, No.607 Sqn, France.

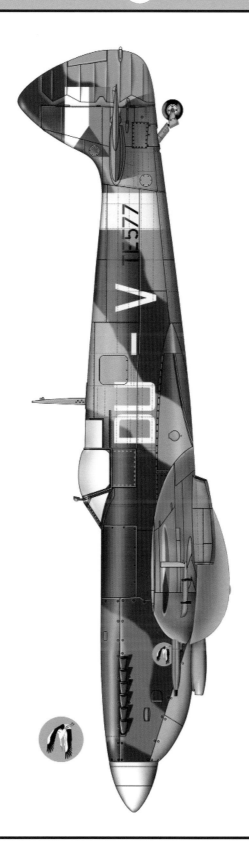

Supermarine Spitfire LF.IXE TE577, No.312 (Czechoslovak) Squadron, Manston, UK, August 1945.
This aircraft is wearing the Czech markings painted just before to make the way back to Prague. It is one of the 76 Spitfires the Czechoslovaks received before returning to their country.

SENIOR OFFICERS WHO FLEW WITH No.312 SQUADRON 1940-1945

BIRD-WILSON, Harold A.C.
6-44/2-45   W/C   RAF
RAF No.40335
Pre-war RAF pilot, who served with No.17 Sqn during the Battle of France and Battle of Britain, but was severely wounded in action on 24.09.40. Returned to combat with No.234 Sqn in March 1941 before taking command of No.152 Sqn in April 1942 and No.66 Sqn the following November. CO No.122 Wing between May 1943 and January 1944. CO of Harrowbeer Wing between June 1944 and February 1945. Remaining with the RAF after the war, he retired as an Air Vice-Marshal in 1974. Nine confirmed victories, six being shared with Nos.17 Sqn and Harrowbeer Wing. DSO [Harrowbeer Wing], DFC [No.17 Sqn] & BAR [No.122 Airfield/Wing].

CERMAK, Jan   W/C   (CZ)/RAF
6-44/7-44   RAF No.84666
See biography p60.

DOLEZAL, Frantisek   W/C   (CZ)/RAF
3-43/2-44   RAF No.82593
Pre-war CzAF fighter pilot in Air Regiment 2. Escaped to France via Poland on 20.06.39. Served with the French in 1940 at GC II/2 claiming three confirmed victories, two being shared. Escaped to England in June 1940. No.310 (Czech) Sqn in August 1940, No.19 Sqn in September 1940, before returning in October to No.310 Sqn until January 1943, then CO between April 1943 - February 1944. Second Czech fighter to be awarded the DSO [Exeter Wing]. Three confirmed, one being shared with Nos.19 and 310 Sqns. DFC [No.310 (Czech) Sqn].

HLADO, Jaroslav   W/C   (CZ)/RAF
11-44/8-45   RAF No.125414
See biography in Squadron pilot roster. Last CO of Czechoslovak Wing in November. Last Czech fighter pilot to be awarded the DSO.

MRAZEK, Karel   W/C   (CZ)/RAF
6-42/3-43   RAF No. 82561
Pre-war CzAF fighter pilot in Air Regiment 2. served with the French in 1940 in a reconnaissance unit before escaping to the United Kingdom. No.310 (Czech) Sqn in August 1940, then with Nos.43 and 46 Sqns between September 1940 and April 1941. Then served briefly with No.257 Sqn, then No.313 (Czech) Sqn between April and June 1942, becoming the CO in December 1941. CO Exeter Wing between June 1942 and April 1943. First Czech fighter pilot to be awarded the DSO [Exeter Wing]. Four confirmed victories, one being shared with Nos.46, 313 Sqn and Exeter Wing, 1940 - 1942. DFC [No.313 (Czech) Sqn].

VYBIRAL, Tomas   W/C   (CZ)/RAF
2-44/11-44   RAF No.83236
See biography in Squadron pilot roster. CO No.134 (Czechoslovak) Wing in 1944. Third Czech fighter pilot ot be awarded the DSO.

DSO : 31.12.42

Wing Commander Karel MRAZEK, D.F.C. (82561), Royal Air Force, Exeter Wing.

This Officer has been the leader od his Wing since June 1942, since when it has destroyed 14 enemy aircraft, probably destroyed 5 more, damaged 15 and carried out many sweeps and offensive operations. Wing Commander Mrazek has throughout shown a very high standard of leadership, both in the air and on the ground, and his personal courage, enterprise and eagerness to engage the enemy have been of the greatest value, as well as an inspiration to his Squadrons. The efficiency of the Wing and its small number of losses are largely due to this gallant Officer´s skillful and accurate leadership.

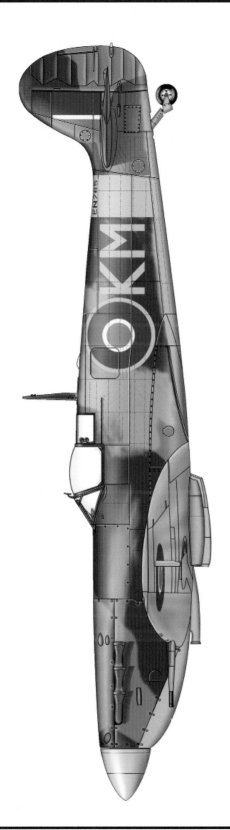

Supermarine Spitfire Mk.VB EN765, Wing Commander Karel Mrazek, Exeter Wing, Exeter, Summer 1942.

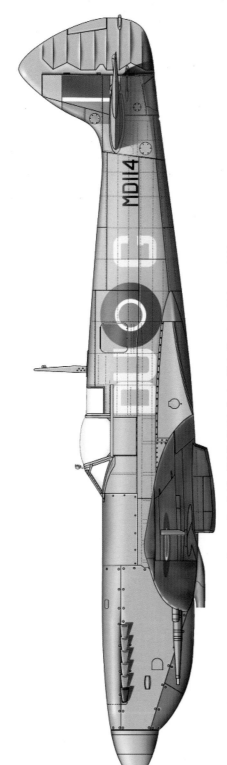

Supermarine Spitfire HF.VII MD114, Station Flight Skaebrae, February 1944.
Although this aircraft is carrying No.312 (Czechoslovak) Squadron's markings, it was never used by this unit.

The squadron had indeed been based at Skaebrae, however it had left in September 1943, and this aircraft was not allotted to the Station Flight until February 1944. This code had been inherited and had been unofficial since the end of 1943 and the beginning of 1944. Indeed is was customary for aircraft, whether Mk V, Mk.VI or Mk.VII, to remain at Skaebrae (allowing for normal rotation of overhauls) and units posted normally consisted of pilots and ground crew who left their original aircraft behind and took over the ones based at Skaebrae. There was a shortage of Spitfire Mk.IXs, which were needed for the 2nd TAF, whereas Orkney was seen to be adequately defended by Mk.Vs and a handful of high altitude marks. While stationed at Skaebrae the Czechs used three Spitfire VIIs (MB763/DU-W, MB765 and MB828).

Whatever the reasons the high-altitude Spitfires retained their DU codes and later there was another Spitfire VII, MD122 which was coded DU-Z. It is believed this situation came about as an oversight by the Squadron which replaced No.312, which then became an entrenched practice. This is probably one of the few cases, if not the only one, when two UK-based RAF fighters units used the same code at the same time.